Stage 3 Paper 9

Financial Reporting

First edition 1996
Fourth edition January 1999

ISBN 0 7517 3478 0 (previous edition 0 7517 3448 9)

British Library Cataloguing-in-Publication Data

A catalogue record for this book
is available from the British Library

Published by

BPP Publishing Limited
Aldine House, Aldine Place
London W12 8AW

http://www.bpp.co.uk

Printed in Great Britain by Ashford Colour Press, Gosport, Hants.

If you use CIMA **Passcards**, you can be sure that the time you spend on final revision for your **1999 exams** is time well spent.

- They **save you time**: following the structure of the BPP Study Text for Paper 9, important facts on key exam topics are summarised for you

- They incorporate diagrams to kick start your memory

- They are pocket-sized: you can run through them **anytime** and **anywhere**

CIMA **Passcards** focus on the exam you will be facing.

- They highlight which topics have been examined - and when

- They provide you with suggestions on subject examinability, given past exams and the direction the examiner appears to be taking, in **exam focus points**

- They give you useful **exam hints** that can earn you those vital extra marks in the exam

Run through the complete set of **Passcards** as often as you can during your final revision period. The day before the exam, try to go through the **Passcards** again. You will then be well on your way to passing your exams. **Good luck!**

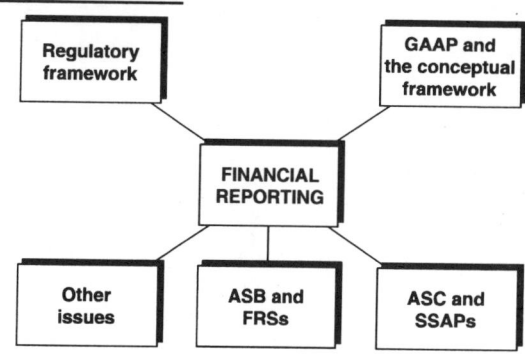

Financial reporting

- The reporting environment changes constantly, through new regulations, standards etc

- International influences on UK reporting are increasing, via IASC and multinational businesses

Regulatory framework

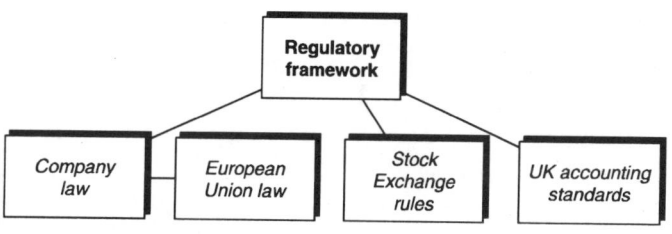

Company law

Consolidated by the Companies Act 1985, updated by the Companies Act 1989. The Acts lay out the formats, contents and rules for the preparation of financial statements.

European Union law

The UK is obliged to comply with legal directives issued by the EU: see Chapter 29.

Stock Exchange rules

The Stock Exchange listing requirements (Yellow Book) must be complied with by companies on the market. The Alternative Investment Market (AIM) has less stringent requirements.

UK accounting standards

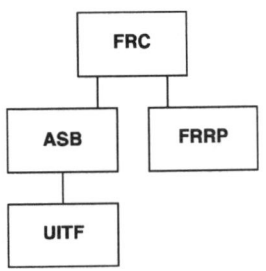

The standard-setting structure is as follows.

- *FRC (Financial Reporting Council)*: umbrella organisation for the standard-setting regime, responsible for financing, enforcement, appointments

- *FRRP (Financial Reporting Review Panel)*: reviews company accounts for non-compliance with accounting standards, truth and fairness, sufficient disclosure etc

- *ASB (Accounting Standards Board)*: produces FRSs from FREDs and DDs (see below)

- *UITF (Urgent Issues Task Force)*: produces 'abstracts' to tackle problem areas quickly (within one month); may be incorporated into subsequent standards; Abstract 7 *True and fair override disclosures* is an important one

GAAP and the conceptual framework

Conceptual framework

- *Definition*: a statement of generally accepted theoretical principles which form the frame of reference for financial reporting

- The previous approach was just to tackle problems as they arose; this caused overlaps, contradictions, loopholes etc

- The IASC's *Framework* document and the *Solomons Report* have been used as a basis for the ASB's *Statement of Principles*

Statement of Principles

- Will provide the conceptual basis for UK standards
- Produced chapter by chapter, currently in ED
- See Chapter 22

GAAP

Generally Accepted Accounting Practice (GAAP) consists of:

- Mandatory sources
  - Company law
  - Accounting standards
  - Stock Exchange requirements

- Non-mandatory sources
  - o IASs
  - o Foreign statutory requirements

GAAP changes constantly.

ASC and SSAPs

- ASC forerunner to ASB

- The main problems of the ASC and SSAPs
  - o The ASC was too open to political lobbying
  - o The SSAPs often allow more than one treatment
  - o There was no conceptual framework
  - o Too many detailed rules led to rigidity

ASB and FRSs

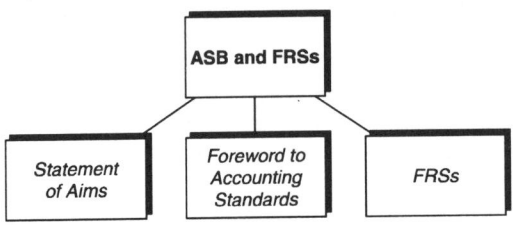

Statement of Aims

- *Aims*: 'to establish and improve standards of financial accounting and reporting, for the benefit of users, preparers and auditors of financial information.'

- *Achieving the aims*
  - o Developing principles to provide a framework
  - o Issuing new standards or amending existing ones

- o Addressing urgent issues promptly

- *Fundamental guidelines*
  1 Objectivity; represent commercial activity
  2 Clear expression; supported by analysis
  3 Inclusion of only properly researched material
  4 Due regard paid to international developments
  5 Consistency between standards and law
  6 Benefits of standards must exceed costs
  7 Evolutionary rather than revolutionary change

Foreword to Accounting Standards

- Standards have force of law

- Compliance with standards necessary to show true and fair view

- Spirit and reasoning of standards should be followed

- Departure is allowed *rarely* to show a true and fair view

- Departures should show true economic effects and be fully disclosed

- DTI and Review Panel have powers of investigation and restatement

FRSs

Financial Reporting Standards (FRSs) are produced after consultation on Financial Reporting Exposure Drafts (FREDs) and, sometimes, Discussion Drafts (DDs).

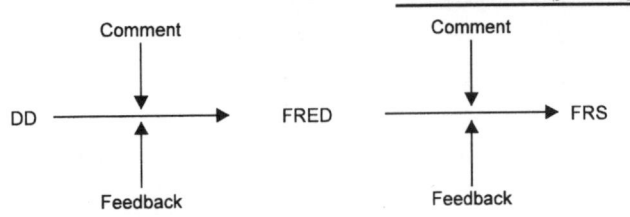

Other issues

Current issues which you should be able to discuss include the following.

- Corporate governance
  - Cadbury Committee
  - Greenbury Report
  - UITF Abstract 10 (directors' share options)
  - Hampel Committee

- Big GAAP/little GAAP and the FRSSE

Exam focus. You must stay up to date for this exam by reading accountancy journals.

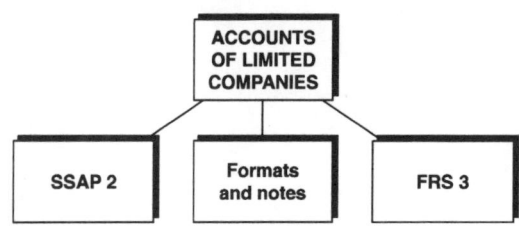

SSAP 2

To understand a set of financial statements, you must be aware of the main assumptions upon which the financial statements are based.

SSAP 2 defines three important terms.

- Fundamental accounting concepts
- Accounting bases
- Accounting policies

You should know these by now.

Fundamental concepts

SSAP 2 deals with the four fundamental concepts:

- The 'going concern' concept
- The 'accruals' concept
- The 'consistency' concept
- The 'prudence' concept

You should know these by now.

Other conventions

- CA 1985 adds the separate valuation principle
- Business entity convention
- Money measurement convention
- Cost convention

Formats and notes

The following gives a typical example of a P&L a/c (operational format) and B/S (vertical format), with the numbered notes which you would normally expect to be present.

PROFIT AND LOSS ACCOUNT
FOR THE YEAR ENDED 31 DECEMBER 19X9

	Notes	£'000	£'000
Turnover	2		X
Cost of sales			X
Gross profit			X
Distribution costs			X
Administrative expenses			X
Operating profit	3		X
Income from other FA investments	6		X
Interest payable & similar charges	7		X
Profit on ordinary activities before tax			X
Tax on profit on ordinary activities	8		X
Profit on ordinary activities after tax			X
Dividends paid and proposed	9	X	
Transfer to general reserve	20	X	
			X
Retained profit for the financial year			X

BALANCE SHEET AS AT 31 DECEMBER 19X9

	Notes	£'000	£'000
Fixed assets			
Intangible assets	10		X
Tangible assets	11		X
Fixed asset investments	12		X
			X
Current assets			
Stocks	13	X	
Debtors	14	X	
Cash at bank and in hand		X	
		X	
Creditors: due < 1 year	15	X	
Net current assets			X
Total assets less current liabilities			X
Creditors: due > 1 year	17		X
Accruals and deferred income	18		X
			X
Capital and reserves			
Called up share capital	19		X
Share premium account	20		X
Revaluation reserve	20		X
General reserve	20		X
Profit and loss account	20		X
			X

Approved by the board on ....
Director ....

The notes on pages 10 to 13 form part of these accounts.

NOTES TO THE ACCOUNTS

1   *Accounting policies*

   (a)   These accounts have been prepared under the historical cost convention of accounting

   (b)   Depreciation is provided on a straight line basis to write off the cost of depreciable fixed assets over their estimated useful lives. Rates used: buildings - X%; plant & machinery - X%; fixtures & fittings - X%

   (c)   Stocks have been valued at the lower of cost and net realisable value

Other policy notes are required on R&D; foreign currency transactions

We are constrained by space from showing all the notes here, but extra information on disclosure of individual items is given throughout these *Passcards*. A summary is given as follows.

2   Breakdown of turnover, PBT and net assets per CA 1985 and SSAP 25 *Segmental reporting*

3   *Operating profit* stated after charging:
       Depreciation
       Amortisation
       Hire of plant and machinery (SSAP 21)
       Auditors' remuneration
       Exceptional items
       Directors' emoluments (see note 4)
       Staff costs (see note 5)
       Research and development

4   *Directors' emoluments*
        Fees
        Other remuneration
        Pensions
        Compensation for loss of office
        Paid to third parties

   Also disclose Chairman's and highest paid director's pay; number of directors with emoluments in bands of £5,000; emoluments waived by directors in year

5   Employee information: average numbers by product, by activity; breakdown of total costs

6   Income from fixed asset investments; split between group undertakings, participating interests and other

7   Interest payable and similar charges: on loans from group undertakings, and other loans/overdrafts

8   Tax on profits on ordinary activities: per SSAP 8 (see Chapter 6)

9   Dividends: preference, ordinary (interim and final)

10   Intangible fixed assets: movements in cost, amortisation and NBV by category

11   Tangible fixed assets: movements in cost, depreciation and NBV by category; details of revaluations

12   Fixed asset investments: movements in shareholdings in group companies, investments etc; AIM not a listed investment; give aggregate market value if material

13   Stocks (see Chapter 5)

14   *Debtors*

    Trade debtors
    Other debtors
    Prepayments and accrued income

    Of this £X of recoverable ACT is recoverable > 1 year

15   *Creditors: due < 1 year*

    Debenture loans: X% stock 19XX
    Bank loans and overdrafts
    Trade creditors
    Other creditors incl tax & social security (see note 16)
    Accruals and deferred income

    Details of security

16   *Other creditors including taxation and social security*

    UK corporation tax
    ACT on dividends
    Other tax and social security
    Other creditors
    Proposed dividend

17   Creditors: due > 1 year: eg loan stock; details of very long term creditors; debentures issued during the year

18   Accruals and deferred income: government grants received less credits to P&L a/c

19   Called up share capital: authorised and allotted ordinary and preference shares; shares issued during year

20   Reserves: movements analysed between share premium, revaluation, general P&L a/c etc

21   Contingent liabilities: see Chapter 11

22   Post balance sheet events: see Chapter 11

23   *Capital commitments*

Contracted but not provided for $\underline{\underline{X}}$

Note only; not in the B/S as just a warning of future expenditure

24   *Significant holdings in other undertakings*

Significant =≥ 20% NV any class of share, *or*
                    ≥ 20% investing co's total assets

Disclose: name of investee co; country of incorporation; description of each class of share held and NV; capital and reserves, profits of investee co for latest year

FRS 3   *5/96, 11/96, 11/97, 5/98*

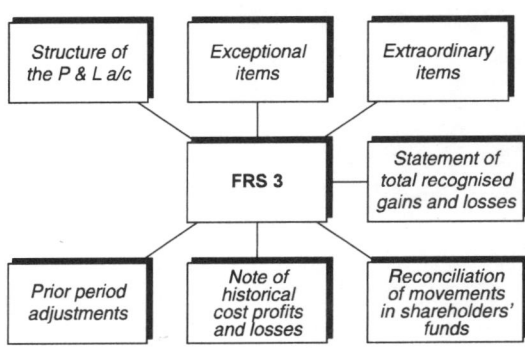

FRS 3 represents an attempt by the ASB to improve financial reporting by addressing a number of major issues.

Structure of the P&L a/c

- All statutory headings from turnover to operating profit are subdivided: continuing vs discontinued operations

- Turnover and operating profit are further analysed: existing vs newly acquired operations

- Only figures for turnover and operating profit need be shown on the face of the P&L a/c; costs etc can be by note

A *discontinued operation* meets *all* these conditions.

- Sale/termination must be completed before the earlier of 3 months after the year end or the date the financial statements are approved (terminations not completed by this date: disclose in the notes)

- Former activity must have ceased permanently

- Sale/termination has a material effect on the nature and focus of the entity's operations and represents a material reduction in its operating facilities resulting from either
  - o Withdrawal from a market (business or geographical)
  - o Material reduction in turnover in its continuing markets

- Assets, liabilities, results of operations and activities are clearly distinguishable, physically, operationally and for financial reporting purposes

Accounting for the discontinuation involves the following.

- The *results of the discontinued operation* up to the date of sale/termination or the B/S date should be shown under each of the relevant P&L a/c headings

- The *profit/loss on discontinuation* or costs of discontinuation should be disclosed separately as an exceptional item after operating profit, before interest

- *Figures for the previous year* must be adjusted for any activities which are now discontinued in the current year

- Once a business is committed to dispose of an operation (eg by signing a sale agreement) it should *provide* for direct costs of sale *or* termination; and any operating losses up to the date of sale/termination

  - If the operation continues during the whole of the accounting period then the provision should be included under the continuing column

  - If the operation is discontinued in the next accounting period, the provision will be utilised and disclosed

---

Exam focus. In 5/96 question 2 asked for the FRS 3 definition of a discontinued operation, which then had to be applied to a given situation.

Acquisitions include:

- Business combinations that are accounted for as mergers or as acquisitions

- Associates that become subsidiaries, on further acquisition of shares

Start-ups and acquisitions of associates are not acquisitions.

Exceptional items

Exceptional items are material items which derive from events or transactions that fall within the ordinary activities of the reporting entity and which need to be disclosed by virtue of their size or incidence if the financial statements are to give a true and fair view. Show on the face of the P&L a/c:

- Profit *and* loss (no offset) on the sale/termination of an operation

- Costs of a fundamental reorganisation or restructuring that has a material effect on the nature and focus of the reporting entity's operations

- Profit *and* loss (no offset) on disposal of fixed assets (difference between sale proceeds and the *carrying value* of the investment)

Other exceptional items should be allocated to the appropriate statutory format heading and attributed to continuing or discontinued operations as appropriate. If sufficiently material (to show a true and fair view), disclose on the face of the P&L a/c.

Extraordinary items

Extraordinary items are material items possessing a *high degree of abnormality* which arise from events or transactions that fall outside the ordinary activities of the reporting entity and which are not expected to recur. Note that ordinary activities *include* infrequent and unusual events.

- Now largely redundant as ASB stated that such items are not expected to appear in P&L a/cs in future

- Should be shown on the face of the P&L a/c before dividends and minority interests; tax and MI in the extraordinary item shown separately; description given in the notes

Statement of total recognised gains and losses   *11/96*

Presented with the same prominence as the P&L a/c, B/S and cash flow, as a primary statement.

- *Contents*

Profit for the year (per P&L a/c)	X
Items taken directly to reserves (*not* goodwill written off to reserves)	
Unrealised surplus on revaluation of fixed assets	X
Surplus/deficit on revaluation of investment properties	X
Currency translation differences on foreign currency net investments	X̲
Total recognised gains and losses for the year	X̄
Prior period adjustments (see later)	(X)̲
Total gains and losses recognised since last annual report	X̳

- Once an unrealised gain or loss is recognised in the statement, transfer for inclusion in the P&L when it becomes realised at a later date is *not* allowed

- Transactions with shareholders are excluded (dividends paid and proposed, share issues, redemptions): these transactions do not represent gains/losses

- Where profit/loss for the year is the only recognised gain/loss, a statement to that effect should be given immediately below the P&L a/c

Reconciliation of movements in shareholders' funds   *11/96*

- In the notes to the accounts *or* a primary statement

- Pulls together financial performance of the entity as it is reflected in
  o   P&L a/c
  o   Other movements in shareholders' funds as in the statement of total recognised gains and losses
  o   All other changes in shareholders' funds not recognised in either of the above

- *Example*

Profit for the financial year	X
* Dividends	(X)
	X
Other recognised gains and losses	X
(per statement of total recognised gains and losses)	
* New share capital	X
Net addition to shareholders' funds	X
Opening shareholders' funds	X
Closing shareholders' funds	X

   * Items not appearing in the primary statements

Exam focus. Question 4 in 11/96 asked for an explanation of the purpose and contribution of both of the above statements, as well as preparation of both. Question 3 in 11/97 asked for the correct treatment, under FRS 3, of three transactions.

Note of historical cost profits and losses

Reported profit ≠ HC profit where alternative accounting rules used. If the difference is material, then include a reconciliation statement after the statement of recognised gains and losses or the P&L a/c. Reconcile profit before tax; however, the retained profit for the year must also be restated.

Prior period adjustments

- *Definition*: material adjustments applicable to prior periods arising from changes in accounting policies or from the correction of fundamental errors; does *not* include normal recurring adjustments or corrections of account estimates made in prior periods

- *Accounting treatment*
  o Restate prior year P&L a/c and B/S
  o Restate opening reserves balance
  o Include in the reconciliation of movements in shareholders' funds
  o Note at the foot of the statement of total recognised gains and losses of the current period

- *Fundamental error*: an error which is so significant that it destroys the truth and fairness of the financial statements

- *Change in accounting policy*: based on the fundamental accounting concept of consistency; reasons for a change in policy
  o Gives fairer presentation of financial position/result
  o Introduction of, or change to standard or legislation

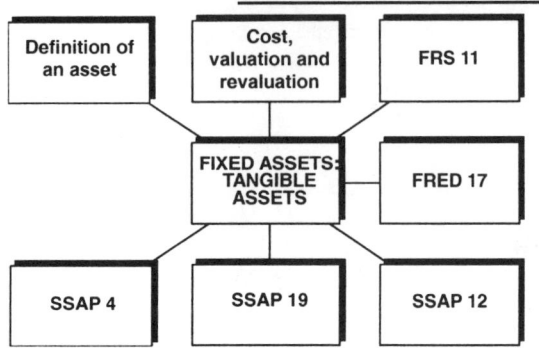

Definition of an asset

- *ASB Statement of Principles*: assets are rights or other access to future economic benefits controlled by an entity as a result of past transactions or events

- *FASB (USA)*: assets are probable future economic benefits obtained or controlled by a particular entity as a result of past transactions or events

- *Key points*
  - Future economic benefit
  - Control
  - Transaction to acquire control has taken place

- *CA 1985 definition of fixed assets:* assets intended for use on a continuing basis in the company's activities

Cost, valuation and revaluation

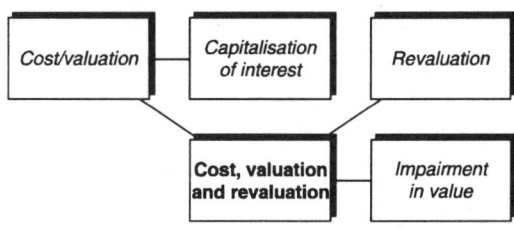

Cost/valuation

According to CA 1985:

- Base *value* on purchase price or cost of production

- May add *expenses* incidental to acquisition

- *Production costs* include raw materials, consumables and other attributable direct costs; may include reasonable proportion of indirect costs; and any interest borrowed to finance production of the asset

Capitalisation of interest   *11/95 , 11/97*

Controversial area. No UK standard at present. Covered by IAS 23.

- *Pros*

  - Borrowing costs are part of total cost in bringing asset into use

  - Capitalisation gives greater comparability between companies: *purchase price* includes interest incurred by seller; *construction cost* would also include interest

- *Cons*
  - o Finance costs are not the most direct of costs, may relate to the business as a whole
  - o Lack of comparability due to different financing policies: businesses with loan financing have higher values for fixed assets than equity-backed businesses

Revaluation   *11/96*

- *CA 1985 alternative accounting rules:* HC principles but permits revaluation and CCA provided that
  - o Items affected and basis of valuation disclosed
  - o HC or difference with revalued amount disclosed

- *Valuation concepts/methods:* CA 1985 allows 3, which overlap (not mutually exclusive)
  - o Current cost
  - o Market value
  - o Directors' valuation

- *FRS 3 rule:* surplus on revaluation *cannot* be taken to the P&L a/c when the asset is sold, but must be transferred via reserves

- *Problem*: allows revaluation of some assets without requiring revaluation of others; result is difficult comparability; solution is FRS 3 note reconciling HC profits to reported profits

---

Exam focus. Part of question 5 in 11/96 asked about accounting for the sale of a revalued asset, in particular about the FRS 3 rule mentioned above. Part of question 5 in 11/97 asked you to compute the cost and depreciation of constructed fixed assets. Capitalisation of borrowing costs was involved.

ASB DD *Role of valuation in financial reporting* would require the following.

- Revaluation of properties (excluding fixed assets specific to the business - not defined)

- Revaluation of quoted investments

- Revaluation of stock of a commodity nature; long-term stock where a market of sufficient depth exists

Impairment in value

CA 1985 requires any *permanent* fall in the value of an asset to be charged against:

- Any revaluation surplus relating to the asset, *and then*
- P&L a/c

A *temporary* fall may be debited to the revaluation reserve, even where there is no existing surplus.

- Now dealt with in FRS 11 on impairment

UITF Abstract 5

- Assets transferred from current to fixed assets must be transferred at realisable value, *not* book value

- Write downs thus taken to P&L, *not* to revaluation reserve

FRS 11

FRS 11 *Impairment of fixed assets and goodwill* sets out the following treatment.

- Only review fixed assets for impairment if there are indications of it, eg

- o Operating loss
- o Decline in market value
- o Change in business environment
- o Change in interest rates, hence recoverable amount
- o Commitment to re-organisation

- If possible test individual fixed assets, otherwise *income generating units*

- Compare *carrying value* with *recoverable amount*, which is the higher of
  - o Net realisable value
  - o Value in use (calculated by discounting expected cash flows from use of asset at market rate)

- Where an acquisition giving rise to goodwill is merged with an existing business, calculate internally generated goodwill in the existing business at the date of the merger. This will be used to calculate any impairment loss in the merged business

- An impairment loss may be reversed if the events giving rise to it reverse

- Generally recognise impairment losses in the P&L

- If it arose on a previously revalued fixed asset, recognise in STRGL but impairments below historical cost are recognised in the P&L

- If impairment loss is caused by a consumption of economic benefits, recognise in the P&L

FRED 17

FRED 17 *Measurement of tangible fixed assets* would require the following.

- *Initial measurement:* cost, written down where necessary to recoverable amount; capitalisation of borrowing costs directly attributable to construction

- *Valuation:* continue present modified HC system; if assets are revalued, all in the class must be and kept systematically up to date; external valuation at least every 5 yrs plus interim internal valuations

- *Depreciation:* all assets depreciated other than freehold land; proper disaggregation of assets to estimate useful economic life. UEL reviewed annually

- *Investment properties:* continue to be exempt from depreciation

SSAP 12   5/98

Definition

Depreciation is the measure of the wearing out, consumption or other reduction in the useful economic life of a fixed asset, whether arising from use, effluxion of time or obsolescence through technology and market changes.

Accounting treatment

- Allocate depreciation to charge fair proportion of cost/valuation less residual value to each accounting period expected to benefit from its use (matching)

- Consider
  - Carrying value of asset (cost of acquisition/production or up to date valuation)
  - Length of useful economic life to present owner

- o Estimated residual value based on prices on acquisition/revaluation

  Method used should be most appropriate to type of asset

- *Revision of useful life*
  - o *Normally* write off NBV over revised remaining useful life
  - o *Except*, if future results would be materially distorted, recognise the cumulative effect in current year (FRS 3)

- *Impairment in value*: NBV not recoverable in full ∴ write down immediately to estimated recoverable amount = *lower* of
  - o Net realisable value
  - o Amount recoverable from further use

- *Change in method of depreciation*: write off net book amount over remaining useful life, using new method

- *Depreciation charge*
  - o P&L a/c: based on value in B/S
  - o No charge taken directly to reserves
  - o No write back of depreciation charged previously
  - o Freehold land does not usually require depreciation
  - o Buildings should be depreciated

- *Disposal of revalued assets*: per FRS 3
  - o Profit or loss = sales proceeds less carrying amount
  - o Revaluation surplus transferred to P&L a/c (realised)

Disclosure

- *For each major class of asset*
  - o Depreciation method
  - o Useful economic lives or depreciation rates

- o Total depreciation charge for period
- o Gross amount of depreciable assets and related accumulated depreciation

- *In year of change/revaluation*
  - o Effect of change in method of depreciation
  - o Effect of revaluation

  on depreciation charge for the year, if material; if change in method, also give reason for the change

SSAP 19   *11/97*

Definition

- An *investment property* is an interest in land and/or buildings in respect of which construction work and development have been completed, *and* which is held for its investment potential, any rental income being negotiated at arm's length

- *Exceptions:* property owned *and* occupied by a company for its own purposes; *and* property let to and occupied by another group company, for both company and group accounts

Accounting treatment

- *Not* depreciated, except leasehold unexpired term < 20 yrs

- *Revalue* each year to open market value

- *Increase* in value goes to Investment Revaluation Reserve (IRR)

- *Diminutions* in value
  - o *Permanent*: charged to P&L a/c
  - o *Temporary*: temporary IRR deficit allowed

- *Disposals*: per FRS 3, as under SSAP 12 above

Disclosures

- Properties and IRR given prominent display

- Names/qualifications of valuers; if employee/officer of company; basis of valuation

- Non-compliance with CA 1985 for true and fair view should be noted

SSAP 4

Problems

- Conflict of accruals vs prudence concepts

- Matching is difficult if it is not clear which expenditure the grant should be applied to

Accounting treatment

- Government grants matched in P&L a/c with expenditure for which they are contributed

- If for fixed assets, grant recognised over useful economic life of asset

- Grants not recognised in P&L a/c until conditions of receipt complied with

- If part or all recognition deferred, treat as deferred income

- Potential liabilities to repay, provided for to the extent repayment probable

Accounting entries

- *Revenue grants*

    Debit   Cash
    Credit   P&L a/c

    In the period in which the related revenue expenditure is charged

- *Capital grants*

    Debit   Cash
    Credit   Deferred income

    On receipt; release to P&L a/c over the expected useful life of the related asset

Disclosure

- Accounting policy note

- Effect of government grants on the results for the period and/or the position at the B/S date

- Potential liability to repay grants disclosed per FRS 12

> *Exam focus.* These standards are quite straightforward, but they may be included as part of a larger question, as happened in 11/97.

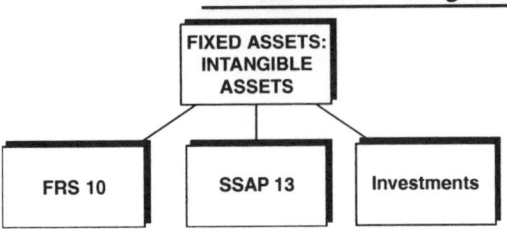

CA 1985: intangible fixed assets in the statutory format consist of:

1   Development costs
2   Concessions, patents, licences, trade marks etc
3   Goodwill
4   Payments on account

Item 4 is covered under stock; item 2 treated as assets if acquired for a consideration; items 1 and 3 covered here.

FRS 10

Under FRS 10 *Goodwill and intangible assets* both purchased goodwill and intangible assets should be *capitalised as assets* in the B/S. Thereafter treatment depends on the nature of investment.

- There is a rebuttable presumption that the useful economic lives (UEL) of purchased goodwill and intangible assets are limited and do not exceed 20 years from acquisition.

- The UEL may be regarded as greater than 20 years or even indefinite, but only if the goodwill is capable of continued measurement so that annual impairment reviews can be performed

- Where goodwill and intangible assets are regarded as having limited UEL they should be amortised

- Where they are regarded as having indefinite UEL they should not be amortised

- Where they are not amortised or are amortised over more than 20 years, impairment reviews should be performed each year

- Negative goodwill should be recognised and separately disclosed on the face of the balance sheet immediately below the goodwill heading. It should be recognised in the profit and loss account in the periods in which the non monetary assets acquired are depreciated or sold

- Internally generated goodwill should not be capitalised and internally developed intangible assets should be capitalised only where they have a readily ascertainable market value

Exam focus. Goodwill is a very important issue in the light of FRS 10. A discussion question was asked in 5/95, and in 11/96 question 1 included a 10 mark (out of 40) discussion on goodwill. In addition, part of question 5 in 11/96 also asked about the capitalisation of an internally-generated brand.

SSAP 13

Problem is one of matching concept vs prudence concept.

Definitions

- *Pure/basic research*: experimental/theoretical work

- *Applied research*: original investigation directed towards a specific practical aim/objective

- *Development*: use of scientific/technical knowledge in order to produce new/substantially improved materials, devices, processes etc

Accounting treatment: pure and applied research

Write off as incurred.

Accounting treatment: development expenditure

Written off in year of expenditure, *except* in certain circumstances when it can be deferred to future periods.

- *Circumstances*: clearly defined project; expenditure separately identifiable; outcome reasonably certain as to technical feasibility and commercial viability; total costs to exceed revenue; resources to complete project

- If deferred, show as intangible asset, amortised

- Amortise from beginning of commercial production, systematically by reference to sales etc

- Review annually; where criteria no longer apply, write off

- R&D fixed assets: capitalise and write off over estimated economic lives

- Apply deferral of costs consistently to all projects

Investments

Characteristic of investments: to generate future economic benefits to the investing enterprise. ED 55 covers investments (but not investment properties). See Chapter 12 on group accounts.

Accounting treatment

- *Fixed asset investments*: at original cost less provision for permanent diminution in value; revaluation to reserve

- *Readily marketable investments* (current assets): at current market value; increase/decrease to P&L a/c

- *Other current assets*: at lower of original cost and NRV, or current cost; if current cost, any increase/decrease to revaluation reserve

- *Disposals*: difference between proceeds and carrying value to P&L a/c, or revaluation surplus to P&L a/c as movement on reserves

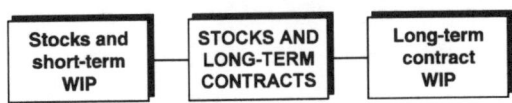

Stocks and short-term WIP   5/96

To comply with the matching concept costs must be allocated between cost of goods sold (matched against current revenues) and closing stock (matched against future revenues).

- Stock should be valued at the lower of cost and NRV

- Costs should include those incurred in the *normal course of business* in bringing a product or service to its *present location and condition*

- *NRV* is the actual or estimated selling price less further costs to be incurred in marketing, selling and distribution

- *Method* used in allocating costs to stock should produce fairest approximation to the expenditure incurred

- Methods include (per CA 1985): average cost, base stock, current cost, FIFO, LIFO, replacement cost, standard cost, unit cost; base stock and LIFO are not allowed under SSAP 9

> *Exam focus.* In 5/96 question 3 on the treatment of stocks in UK accounts had to be compared with the US treatment.

NRV < cost

Principal situations where NRV < cost:

- Increase in costs or fall in selling price
- Physical deterioration of stocks

- Obsolescence of products
- Company decision to make and sell at a loss
- Errors in production or purchasing

Long-term contract WIP   5/95, 11/95

Definition

A *contract* entered into for the construction of a *single substantial asset* where the time taken substantially to complete the contract is such that the contract activity falls into *different accounting periods* (not always > 1 year long).

General accounting treatment

- Recognise turnover and profit as the contract progresses; turnover determined in a manner appropriate to the stage of completion of the contract, the business and industry

- Recognised profit is that part of the total profit currently estimated to arise over the duration of the contract that fairly reflects the profit attributable to that part of the work performed at the accounting date

Attributable profit calculation

Prudence: no attributable profit until profitable outcome of the contract assessed with some certainty. SSAP 9 does not specify; use any method considered reasonable by directors.

- Use % completion basis, on the assumption that profit accrues evenly over the contract. Two common methods
  - *Work certified basis*

    $$\frac{\text{Work certified to date}}{\text{Total contract value}} \times \text{Total estimated profit}$$

o   *Cost basis*

$$\frac{\text{Costs incurred to date}}{\text{Total estimated costs}} \times \text{Total estimated profit}$$

- *Foreseeable losses* are losses currently estimated to arise over the duration of the contract; this estimate is required irrespective of

    o   Whether or not work has yet commenced

    o   Proportion of work carried out at the accounting date

    o   Amount of profit expected to arise on other contracts

- *Problems*

    o   CA 1985 requires attributable profit to be included in debtors, not WIP; may be misleading

    o   SSAP 9 does not

        –   Specify exactly the amounts to be recorded under turnover, or for attributable profit

        –   Define turnover and related costs

        –   Address capitalisation of interest on long-term contract borrowings

Summary of accounting treatment

- *During the year*

    o   *Costs incurred*

        Debit   Contract account (WIP)
        Credit   Cash/creditors

    o   *Progress payments invoiced*

        Debit   Trade debtors
        Credit   Debtors: amounts recoverable on contracts

- o *Cash received*

  Debit Bank
  Credit Trade debtors

- *At year end*

  - o *Turnover recognised*

    Debit Debtors: amounts recoverable on contracts
    Credit Turnover (P&L a/c)

  - o *Costs matched against turnover*

    Debit Cost of sales (P&L a/c)
    Credit Contract account

  - o *Provision for future losses*

    Debit Provisions on long-term contracts (P&L a/c)
    Credit Provision for future losses (B/S)

    Provision is released as contract progresses and loss 'crystallises'

P&L a/c

- *Turnover and cost*

  - o Turnover and associated costs recorded in the P&L a/c 'as contract activity progresses'
  - o Include 'appropriate proportion of total contract value as turnover' in P&L a/c
  - o Costs incurred in reaching that stage of completion are matched with this turnover
  - o Turnover is the 'value of work carried out to date'

- *Attributable profit*

  - o It must reflect the proportion of work carried out
  - o It should take into account any known inequalities in profitability in the various stages of a contract

Balance sheet

- *Stocks and WIP*

Cost to date	X
Less transfers to P&L a/c	(X)
	X
Less foreseeable losses	(X)
	X
Less payments on account in excess of turnover	(X)
WIP	X

- *Debtors*

Cumulative turnover recognised	X
Less payments on account	X
Amount recoverable on contracts	X

- *Creditors*: to the extent payments on account exceed both cumulative turnover and net WIP = payments on account

- *Provisions*: to the extent foreseeable future losses exceed WIP

Exam focus. Discussions on, and calculations of, long-term contracts appeared in both the 5/95 and 11/95 exams. The examiner is keen on topics, such as this one, which have been studied at Stage 2 as well as Stage 3 - and you are expected to do well in them.

SSAP 8 5/96, 5/97

Companies pay CT at 31%, usually 9 months after the financial year end.

> *Exam focus.* From May 1999 advance corporation tax (ACT), which is to be abolished, will no longer be examined. SSAP 8 has not yet been amended, but will be in due course. This change makes this topic much simpler.

- *P&L a/c disclosure*
    - Tax charge, made up and disclosed as follows.

UK corporation tax (at X% on taxable profit)	X
Under/(over) provision in previous years	X
Transfer to/(from) deferred taxation account	$\underline{X}$
	$\underline{\underline{X}}$

- *B/S disclosure*
    - CT liability: under other creditors including tax and social security; may be two liabilities, < and > 1 year

Deferred taxation   S/96, S/97

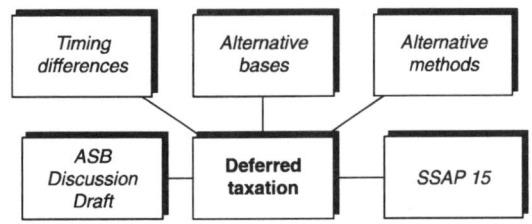

The tax charge in the P&L a/c is often different from the profit before tax figure because of the differences which exist between tax rules and financial accounting principles.

- *Permanent differences* arise where certain items in the P&L a/c are either not taxable or not allowable

- *Timing differences* arise where the items are taxable/ allowable but are dealt with in the tax computation in periods different from those in which they are included in the financial statements

Deferred tax is the tax attributable to timing differences.

Timing differences

- *Short-term timing differences*: result from the fact that certain items of income/expenditure are dealt with on a receipts/payments basis for tax purposes and on an accruals basis for accounts purposes

- *Accelerated capital allowances*: capital allowances are available at a rate higher than the depreciation rate applied to the fixed asset

- *Revaluations*: gains on the increase in value of an asset will only be taxed on sale; the timing difference is the estimated chargeable gain (revalued amount less original cost); if rollover relief is available, the gain will never be taxed so this will then be a permanent difference, not a timing difference

Alternative bases

- *Nil provision*: no provision for deferred tax is made as only the tax payable in respect of a period should be charged

- *Full provision*: timing differences provided for in full, as should recognise tax effects of all transactions in the period

- *Partial provision*: deferred tax accounted for in respect of the net amount by which it is probable that any payment of the tax will be temporarily deferred or accelerated by the operation of timing differences, which will reverse in the foreseeable future without being replaced

Alternative methods

- *Deferral method*: tax effects of timing differences are calculated using tax rates current when differences arise

- *Liability method*: deferred tax provisions are calculated at the rate at which it is estimated that tax will be paid (or recovered) when the timing differences reverse

Liability method is consistent with the aim of partial provision.

SSAP 15

- Provide for deferred tax under the *liability method* on the partial provision basis, ie to the extent that it is probable the liability/asset will crystallise

- Deferred tax *net debit balances* should not be carried forward, *except* to the extent that they are expected to be recoverable without replacement by equivalent debit balances

- *Losses* should be offset within the deferred tax account

  o Calculate provision required for other timing differences in normal manner

  o Offset unrelieved trading losses carried forward against *appropriate elements* of deferred tax balance in this provision

  o The transfer to/from the P&L a/c in respect of deferred tax is the movement in this net balance

- Exceptionally, the tax effect of unrelieved losses may be carried forward as a net debit balance (deferred tax asset) under certain profitability criteria

SSAP 15 requires the following disclosures.

- *B/S*

  o *Deferred tax balance*, its major components: B/S or note

  o *Transfers* to/from deferred tax: note

  o *Show* separately movements to/from deferred tax which arise relating to *movements on reserves* (eg on disposal of revalued assets)

  o Total amount of any *unprovided deferred tax* analysed into major components: note

  o Show the potential amount of deferred tax on a *revalued asset*, which is not shown because the revaluation does not constitute a timing difference, and state the fact

- o Where the value of an asset is shown in a note because it *differs materially from its book amount*, the note should also show the tax effects (if any) arising *if the asset were realised* at the B/S date at the noted value

- *P&L a/c*

  - o Show deferred tax relating to *ordinary activities* separately as a part of the tax on profit/loss on ordinary activities: in P&L a/c or note

  - o Show separately deferred tax relating to any *extraordinary items* as part of tax on extraordinary items; in P&L a/c or note

  - o Disclose amount of any *unprovided deferred tax* in respect of the period analysed into its major components: note

  - o Adjustments to deferred tax arising from *changes in tax rates and tax allowances* should normally be disclosed separately as part of the tax charge for the period; however the effect of a change in the basis of taxation, or in Government fiscal policy, is treated as an extraordinary item where material

---

Exam focus. Question 4 in 5/97 asked for a computation of the tax charge and of the deferred tax under the partial and full provision methods. You were also asked why SSAP 15 prefers the partial provision method.

ASB Discussion Draft

Disadvantages of SSAP 15 include:

- Inconsistent with other standards/international practice: requires deferred tax to be recognised only when it is *not* expected to be permanent feature of the B/S

- Requires estimation of future transactions (against *Statement of Principles*)

Draft recommends new FRS to replace SSAP 15, but the proposals are very tentative; the paper looks at:

- Flow-through (nil provision)
- Partial provision
- Full provision

Full provision is recommended, possibly modified by discounting (taking account of the timing of cash flows); consistent with international practice.

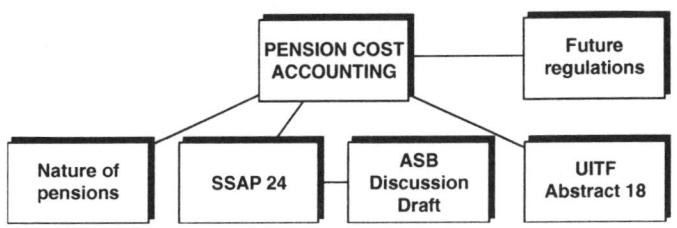

Nature of pensions

Difficulties of accounting for pensions costs in employer's a/cs.

- Amounts involved are large
- Time scale is long
- Estimation process is complex
- Assumptions required in many areas of uncertainty
- Choice of matching principles applied is complex

Accounting objective: employer should recognise the cost of providing pensions on a systematic basis over the period during which receives benefit from the employees' services.

SSAP 24   *6/96, 11/98*

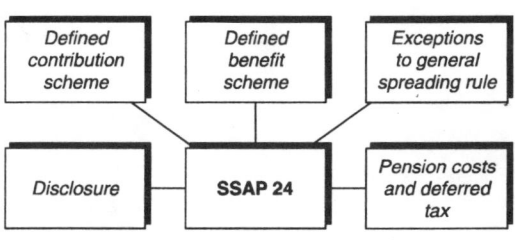

Defined contribution scheme

- *Definition*: a pension scheme in which the benefits are directly determined by the value of contributions paid

- *Rate* of contribution specified in rules of scheme

- *Cost* of scheme known and fixed from the outset

- *Accounting treatment*: charge contributions payable in respect of that accounting period; if amounts paid are more/less than amounts payable, then a prepayment/ accrual will appear

Defined benefit scheme

- *Definition*: a pension scheme in which the rules specify the benefits to be paid; the scheme is financed accordingly

- *Cost*: made up of two elements: regular costs and variations from regular cost

- *Role of actuary*: value the pension fund (assets *and* liabilities); determine the contributions required; devise funding plans to eliminate deficit/surplus

- *Regular cost*: amount the actuary regards as sufficient contribution to provide eventual pensions to be paid in respect of future service, *provided* assumptions prove correct and no further changes; expressed as % of pensionable earnings

- *Variations from regular cost*: arise because of 'unknowns'
  - Valuation of the pension liabilities
  - Valuation of the assets out of which the liabilities paid

- *Role of accountant*: to determine the appropriate accounting treatment

- o *Regular costs*: take to the P&L a/c (matching concept)
- o *Variations from regular cost*: depends on circumstances; variation *usually* spread over the remaining service life of the employees

Exceptions to general spreading rule

- Reductions in employees arising from the *closure of a business segment*: include as part of the exceptional item

- Reduction in employees *not* arising from the closure of a business segment: recognise when the reduction in contributions occurs

- *Refunds* from the scheme: *may* recognise as income in the period of receipt (not required)

- *Increases to pensions* in payment or deferred pensions: recognise immediately

- *Material deficits* recognised over a shorter period: for prudence, where large extra contributions required for deficiency arising from an event outside the scope of normal actuarial assumptions, eg fraud (Maxwell)

- *Discretionary* and *ex-gratia* pension increases and *ex-gratia* pensions (ie unplanned): full capitalised value provided for in year in which they are made; to the extent this exceeds existing surplus, charge to current P&L a/c

Pension costs and deferred tax

- *Timing difference*: if there are variations from regular cost, the pensions paid in an accounting period will not be the same as the amount charged to the P&L a/c ∴ a timing difference arises as tax relief is given on the amount paid: cumulative timing difference = asset/liability in the B/S

- *Provision*: deferred tax on pension costs is provided on a full provision basis

Disclosure

Very detailed, particularly for defined benefit schemes.

- *Nature* of the scheme (defined benefit/contribution)
- Whether it is *funded* or *unfunded*
- *Accounting policy* and, if different, the *funding policy*
- Whether the pension cost and provision (or asset) are assessed by a qualified actuary, and if so, *the date of the most recent formal actuarial valuation* or later formal review used for this purpose (disclose if the actuary is an employee/officer of the company)
- *Pension cost charge* for the period; explanations of significant changes in the charge vs previous period
- Any *provisions* or *prepayments* in the B/S resulting from a difference between the amounts recognised as cost and the amounts funded or paid directly
- Amount of *any deficiency on a current funding level basis*, indicating the action, if any, being taken to deal with it in the current and future accounting periods
- *An outline of the results of the most recent formal actuarial valuation* or later formal review
  - Actuarial method used and a brief description of the main actuarial assumptions
  - Market value of scheme assets at the date of their valuation or review
  - Level of funding expressed in % terms
  - Comments on any material actuarial surplus or deficiency indicated by the funding level

- Any commitment to make *additional payments* over a limited number of years

- Accounting treatment adopted in respect of a refund made where a credit appears in the financial statements in relation to it

- Details of the expected effects on future cost of any material changes in the group's and/or company's pension arrangements

---

Exam focus. Question 5 in 5/96 asked about different types of scheme, the objective of SSAP 24 and the difficulties in satisfying this when dealing with a defined benefit scheme. Calculations were then required for P&L a/c and B/S figures.

ASB Discussion Draft

Criticisms of SSAP 24:

- Too much scope for employers to adjust pension costs in the short term

- Too flexibile, compounded by inadequate disclosure requirements for pension costs and related balances

Main problem with pension costs: the pension cost for a year cannot be known until all current/former employees have died, ie it must be estimated. Two approaches:

- Actuarial approach (preferred)
- Market-based approach (alternative, minority preferred)

Actuarial approach involves the following proposals.

- Use of an accrued benefits actuarial method

- Cost of real improvements to benefits for former employees should be accounted for in the year the awards are made

- Cost of real improvements to benefits for current employees should be spread forward over their remaining service lives

- An experience surplus/deficiency (assumptions proved wrong) and the cost of past-service awards to current employees should be amortised on a straight-line basis

New, clearer disclosures are also suggested.

UITF 18 Abstract 18

UITF Abstract 18 is called *Pension costs following the 1997 tax changes in respect of dividend income.*

Loss to pension schemes arising from abolition of reclaimable tax credit on dividends to be spread forward over expected remaining service lives of current employees.

Future regulations

- Recent scandals include
  o Maxwell, MGN Fund: used fund money to support shares
  o Hanson, Imperial Group Pension Fund: failed to obtain cash repayment after disposing of the business

- Problems
  o Trust law
  o Use of surpluses by companies

- Pensions Act 1995: designed to address the above
  o Minimum Funding Requirement for all final salary schemes
  o One third of trustees must be elected by the members
  o Compensation Scheme for insolvent employers

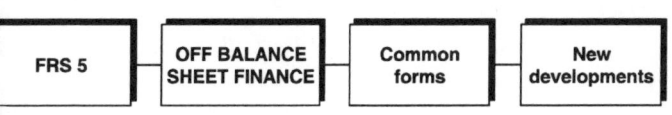

Off balance sheet finance

Definition

The funding or refinancing of a company's operations in such a way that, under legal requirements and existing accounting conventions, some or all of the finance may not be shown on its balance sheet.

Perceived benefits

- *Stock market advantages*: lower gearing ratio

- Keep a company within *loan covenants*

- Exclude highly geared subsidiary from consolidation for reasons of dissimilar activities and thereby reduce gearing

- Expectation of rights issue (to reduce gearing) decreased, thereby maintaining share price

Substance over form

- *Definition*: transactions and other events should be accounted for and presented in accordance with their substance and financial reality and not merely with their legal form (IAS 1)

- *Examples*
  - *SSAP 21:* leases
  - *SSAP 9*: long-term contract, taking attributable profit
  - *FRS 2:* definition and treatment of subsidiaries

Window dressing

Arranging transactions, the substance of which is primarily to alter the appearance of the B/S; *not* falsification of accounts. SSAP 17 (covered in Chapter 11) does allow window dressing but *disclosure* should be made of such transactions.

FRS 5   *11/96*

Statement of Principles, Chapter 2: accounting for items according to substance and economic reality and not merely legal form is a key determinant of reliable information.

- *Majority of transactions:* no difference, so no issue

- *Other transactions:* substance and form diverge; choice of treatment can give different results due to non-recognition of an asset/liability even though benefits/obligations result

Determining the substance of transactions

Does the transaction change the existing assets/liabilities of the company, either by creating new ones or altering the existing ones?

Assets and liabilities

- *Assets*: rights or other access to future economic benefits controlled by an entity as a result of past transactions or events

- *Liabilities*: an entity's obligation to transfer economic benefits as a result of past transactions or events

Recognition

The process of incorporating an item into the primary financial statements with appropriate headings. It involves depiction of the item in words and by monetary amount and the inclusion of that amount in the statement totals.

Derecognition

Where circumstances change, should an asset/liability be removed from the B/S, eg has an asset been sold or has it been used to secure borrowings?

- *Complete derecognition:* all *significant* risks/benefits transferred

- *No derecognition:* either the risks or benefits or both have been retained

- *Partial derecognition:* some transfer of risks/benefits
  - Where an asset has been subdivided
  - Where an item is sold for less than its full life
  - Where an item is transferred for its full life but some risk/benefit is retained

Linked presentation

Non-recourse finance is shown in the B/S as a deduction from the asset to which it relates.

Offset

Offset is only allowed where the debit and credit balances are not really separate assets/liabilities. Can the entity enforce the right of set-off? Criteria:

- Determinable monetary amounts owed

- Entity can insist on/enforce a net settlement

- Net settlement assured beyond doubt (debit before credit)

Process of enquiry

- Has a transaction taken place?

- Has the transaction led to access to future benefits and is the entity exposed to the risks in those benefits?

- Is the asset controlled by the entity?

- Is there sufficient evidence of the existence of the item?

- Can the item be measured as a monetary amount with reasonable reliability?

Common forms

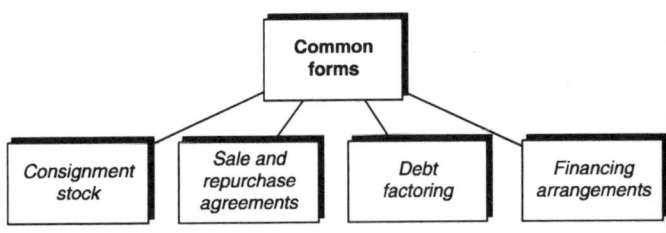

FRS 5's application notes cover some common forms of off balance sheet finance. *Full disclosure* is always required.

Consignment stock   *11/96*

This is stock held by one party (dealer) but owned by another (manufacturer).

- Where stock is *not* an asset of the dealer at delivery

  o *Indications*

    – Manufacturer can require stock return
    – Dealer can return stock easily
    – Manufacturer bears obsolescence risk

- Transfer price = list price at date title passes
- Manufacturer bears slow movement risk

- o *Accounting treatment*

  - Stock not included in dealer's B/S
  - Deposits included in 'other debtors'

- Where stock *is* an asset of the dealer at delivery
  - o *Indications*

    - Manufacturer cannot require stock return
    - Dealer has no right to return stock
    - Dealer bears obsolescence risk
    - Transfer price = list price at delivery
    - Dealer bears slow movement risk

  - o *Accounting treatment*

    - Stock recognised on dealer's B/S
    - Deduct deposits from liability; excess is creditor

Exam focus. Question 3 in 11/96 asked about the general principles of FRS 5 and then a consignment stock transaction.

Sale and repurchase agreements

Company sells an asset to another on terms that allow the company to repurchase the asset in certain circumstances.

- Where there is a sale of the original asset to a buyer (seller may retain different asset)
  - o *Indications*

    - No commitment for seller to repurchase
    - Risk of changes in asset value borne by buyer
    - Asset will be used over life of agreement

- o *Accounting treatment* (sale and leaseback)

    - No profit recognised
    - No adjustment to carrying value of asset

- o *Accounting treatment* (seller has a *new asset/liability,* eg a call option to repurchase the original asset): recognise the new asset or liability per SSAP 18

- Where there is no sale of original asset to buyer (secured loan)

    - o *Indications*

        - Sale price $\neq$ MV
        - Commitment for seller to repurchase asset
        - Risk of changes in asset borne by seller
        - Seller retains right to determine asset use/profits

    - o *Accounting treatment*

        - Seller continues to recognise asset and record the proceeds received as a liability

        - Interest, however designated, should be accrued

        - Carrying amount of asset should be monitored, provide if necessary

Debt factoring   *5/98, 11/98*

The original creditor sells the debts to a factor.

- Where debts are *not* an asset of seller

    - o *Indications*

        - Transfer for single non-returnable sum
        - No recourse to seller for losses
        - Seller has no rights to further sums from factor

- *Accounting treatment: derecognition*

    - Remove debtors from B/S

    - Recognise no liability on receipt of proceeds

    - Profit/loss is the difference between carrying value of debts and amount received

- Where debts *are* an asset of the seller

    o *Indications*

        - Finance cost varies with speed of debt collection

        - Full recourse to seller for losses

        - Seller required to repay amounts from factor on/before set date

    o *Accounting treatment: separate presentation*

        - Gross amount of debts shown in B/S
        - Liability shown for proceeds received
        - Interest element reflected as it accrues
        - Other factoring costs accrued
        - Notes disclose amount of factored debt

- A *linked presentation* may be appropriate

    o *Indications*

        - Some non-returnable proceeds
        - Seller/factor has right to further sums
        - No recourse for losses or fixed monetary ceiling
        - Factor only paid out of amounts collected
        - Seller has no right/obligation to repurchase debt

    o *Accounting treatment*

        - Non-returnable proceeds deducted from gross amount of factored debts

        - Interest element recognised as accrued

Financing arrangements

- Includes securitisation of assets and loan transfers

- Usually liability in company balance sheet - obligation to transfer economic benefits

- If restricted to fixed amount based on performance of asset financed, linked presentation is appropriate

New developments

Discounting

ASB issued working paper on *Discounting in financial reporting*

Establishes general principles on how discounting should be applied so that new FRSs apply it consistently. Aspects discussed are

UITF 13 Accounting for ESOP Trusts

Assets and liabilities of ESOP Trusts should be brought on to the B/S of the sponsoring company if it has *de facto* control over the shares held by the trust.

Exam focus. The examiner is fond of FRS 5 and has expressed disappointment that students seemed unfamiliar with this standard which is by no means new.

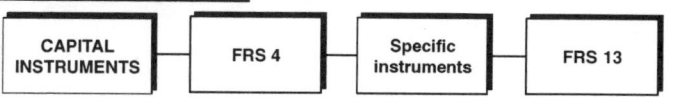

Capital instruments

Because of inherent difficulties in this complex area, it is increasingly difficult for users to assess the nature, amount and cost of a company's debt and equity resources.

FRS 4   *5/95, 11/97, 5/98, 11/98*

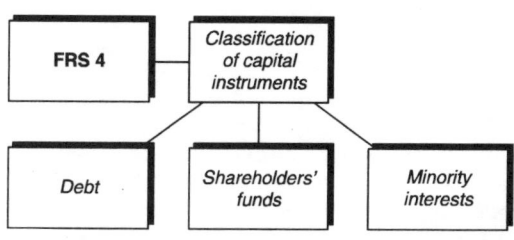

A *capital instrument* is any instrument issued by reporting entities as a means of raising finance including shares, debentures, loans and debt instruments, options and warrants that give the holder the right to subscribe for or obtain capital instruments. Great range available, including convertible bonds, deep discount bonds, stepped interest bonds etc.

Classification of capital instruments

- *Issue*: gearing ratio is only meaningful if consistency in allocation of financial instruments between debt and equity

- *Categories*: debt finance; shareholders' funds; minority interests

Debt

Capital instruments should be classified as liabilities if they contain an obligation to transfer economic benefits as a result of past transactions or events (per *Statement of Principles*).

- *Carrying amount*
  - Immediately after issue, net proceeds = FV of the consideration received after deduction of issue costs
  - Increase by the finance cost in respect of the reporting period and reduce by payments made in respect of the debt in that period

- *Finance charge*: servicing cost of capital instruments allocated to accounting periods so as to achieve a constant rate on the outstanding amount in each period

- *Disclosure*
  - *Maturity of debt*: analysis of maturity showing amounts due: < 1 year/on demand, 1-2 years, 2-5 years, 5+ years
  - *Convertible debt*: stated separately from other liabilities: date of redemption; amount then payable; number and class of shares; period in which may occur; option of issuer/holder

- *Repurchase own debt*: recognise any profit/loss in year of repurchase

Shareholders' funds

- B/S should show the amount of shareholders' funds attributable to both equity and non-equity interests

- *Non-equity shares* are those with limited rights to dividend or a surplus on a winding up, or which are redeemable at the option of the holder; treatment of the carrying value and the finance charge are as for debt *except* the finance cost should be reported as an appropriation of profit

- *Disclosure*
  - Analysis of shares between equity and non-equity interests
  - Rights of each class of shares summarised: to dividends, dates of redemption and amounts payable; priority/amounts receivable on winding up; voting rights
  - Where warrants or convertible debt are in issue that may require the company to issue shares of a class not currently in issue, details as for non-equity shares
  - Aggregate dividends for each class of shares should be disclosed

Minority interests

Those shares which are held by non-group companies will normally be treated as *minority interests* split between equity and non-equity interests. FRS 4 requires that in some cases that they be treated as liabilities, where there is an *obligation* for any group company to transfer economic benefit.

> *Exam focus.* FRS 4 has come up in each of the sittings 11/97 to 11/98. The examiner obviously 'has a thing' about it and expressed disappointment that the questions were not well answered.

Specific instruments

A few examples are given here.

Debt issued with warrants

- Issue is made for the par value and the debt will be redeemed at the same amount

- The warrants and the debts are capable of being transferred separately

- *Required accounting*
  - Recorded at the net proceeds of the issue as part of shareholders' funds
  - When a warrant is exercised the amount previously recognised in respect of the warrant should be included as part of the net proceeds of the shares issued
  - When a warrant lapses the amount previously recognised should be transferred to reserves and reported in the statement of total recognised gains and losses

Deep discount bonds   *11/95*

- Bonds that carry a low nominal rate of interest and $\therefore$ issued at a discount to the value at which they will be redeemed

- Cost to borrower = discount on issue + interest payments

- Such bonds are *liabilities* of the issuer

- *Finance costs* = difference between net proceeds and total payments made, allocated to periods at a constant rate on the carrying amount

- Carrying amount of bond immediately prior to redemption = amount at which it is to be redeemed

- Discount should *not* be treated as an asset

> *Exam focus.* Question 4 in 11/95 required the calculation of the finance charge on a zero-coupon bond (the extreme type of deep discount bond) in relation to the capitalisation of borrowing costs.

Scrip dividends

If shares are issued in lieu of dividends, the value of the shares issued, being equal to the value of the dividend payable, should be reflected in the P&L a/c as an appropriation of profit

Convertible debt

- Conversion of debt should not be anticipated; report in liabilities with the finance cost calculated on the assumption that the debt will never be converted

- When the debt is converted, the amount of consideration recognised in respect of shares should be the amount of the liability for the debt at the date of conversion

Calculations

The method used in the following example applies to deep discount bonds, debt issued with warrants and other similar instruments (including zero coupon bonds).

Debt issued for £400,000 (nominal) on 1.1.19X1 for proceeds of £315,526
Debt redeemed for £400,000 (ie par) on 31.12.19X5
Interest rate = 4%
IRR (may have to calculate) = 9.5%

	£
Annual interest payments (4% × £400,000 × 5)	80,000
Deep discount £(400,000 − 315,526)	84,474
	164,474

At inception:	DEBIT	Cash	£315,526	
	CREDIT	Liability		£315,526

Year	P&L a/c charge * £	Actual interest payable £	Rolled up interest charged to P&L a/c (c) £	Liability in closing B/S £
19X1	29,975	16,000	13,975	329,501
19X2	31,303	16,000	15,303	344,804
19X3	32,756	16,000	16,756	361,560
19X4	34,348	16,000	18,348	379,908
19X5	36,092	16,000	20,092	400,000
	164,474	80,000	84,474	

* $0.095 \times £315,526 = £29,975$
 $0.095 \times £329,501 = £31,303$
 $0.095 \times £344,804 = £32,756$
 $0.095 \times £361,560 = £34,348$
 $0.095 \times £379,908 = £36,092$

FRS 13

FRS 13 *Derivatives and other financial instruments: disclosures* requires companies to provide information on:

- Impact of financial instruments on its risk profile

- How risks arising from financial instruments might affect the entity's performance

- How the risks are being managed

Narrative disclosures

- Role of financial instruments in creating or changing risk

- Directors' approach to managing each risk, including any changes in objectives or policies

- Narrative disclosures are mandatory, but may be given in statement accompanying the financial statements, eg directors' report or operating and financial review

Numerical disclosures

- Different disclosures required for:
  - Entities that are not financial instruments
  - Banks and similar institutions
  - Other financial institutions

- Disclosures required about:
  - Interest rate risk
  - Currency risk
  - Liquidity risk
  - Fair values
  - Financial instruments used for trading
  - Financial instruments used for hedging
  - Certain commodity contracts

- Aggregation is encouraged, to avoid excessive detail

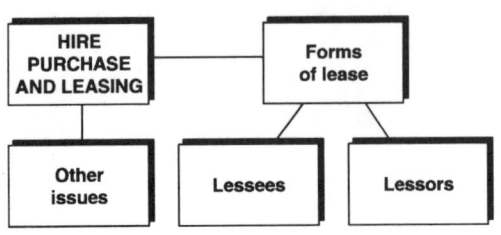

Forms of lease   *11/95, 11/98*

Finance lease

- Transfers substantially all the risks and rewards of ownership of an asset to the lessee

- Presumed if at the inception of a lease the PV of the minimum lease payments ≥ 90% of the FV of leased asset

- *PV*: calculate using the interest rate implicit in the lease

- The minimum lease payments are the minimum payments over the remaining part of the lease term *(except charges for services and taxes to be paid by the lessor) and*

   o   (Lessee) any residual amounts guaranteed by him, *or*

   o   (Lessor) any residual amounts guaranteed by the lessee or by an independent third party

- *Lease term*: the period for which the lessee has contracted to lease the asset (primary *and* secondary periods)

Operating lease

A lease other than a finance lease.

> *Exam focus.* Leasing came up as part of a question on the 11/98 paper.

Lessees

Accounting treatment

- *Finance lease*: record as an asset and obligation at the present value of the minimum lease payments
  - o Depreciate the asset over the shorter of the lease term and its useful life
  - o A finance charge is made to produce a constant periodic rate of charge on the outstanding lease obligation (use actuarial method before tax and sum of the digits method)

- *Operating lease*: rentals charged on a straight-line basis over the lease term

Disclosure

- *Leased assets: either*
  - o Gross/accumulated depreciation for each major class of asset, *or*
  - o Include with owned assets but disclose the net amount of leased assets in overall total

- *Leasing obligations*
  - o Disclose separately
  - o Give maturity analysis (< 1 year; 2-5 years; thereafter)

- *Operating leases*: disclose payments which lessee is committed to make *during the next year* analysed between land and buildings and other assets, for leases expiring < 1 year, 2-5 years, thereafter

- *P&L a/c*
  - o Depreciation charge on leased assets
  - o Finance charge on leasing obligations

- o Operating lease rentals charged: hire of plant and machinery; other
- o Accounting policy

All above disclosures include HP contracts classified as finance/operating leases as appropriate.

Lessors

Accounting treatment

- Net investment in finance leases = debtor

- Allocate earnings so as to give a constant periodic rate of return on the lessor's *net cash investment* in the lease (using the post tax actuarial method)

- *Net cash investment* in a lease at a point in time is the amount of funds invested in a lease by a lessor, comprising the cost of the asset plus or minus the following related payments/receipts

  - o Government/other related grants receivable (-)
  - o Rentals received (-)
  - o Taxation payments/receipts, capital allowances (+/-)
  - o Residual values, if any, at the end of the lease term (-)
  - o Interest payments (where applicable) (+)
  - o Interest received on cash surplus (-)
  - o Profit taken out of the lease (+)

- Assets held for use in operating leases by a lessor are recorded as a fixed asset and depreciated over useful life

Disclosure

- Net investment at B/S date in
  - Finance leases
  - HP contracts

- Gross amounts/accumulated depreciation of assets held for use in operating leases

- Aggregate rentals receivable for the year for
  - Finance leases
  - Operating leases

- Cost of assets acquired for letting under finance leases

Other issues

Sale and leaseback transactions

- If leaseback transaction is a *finance lease*, defer book profit/loss and amortise over shorter of lease term and useful life:

  Profit = accruals and deferred income

  Loss = prepayments and accrued income

- Alternatively, do not recognise disposal has occurred; *Debit* Cash, *Credit* Lessor obligation, with funds raised

- If leaseback transaction is an *operating lease*; where BV = book value; SP = sale proceeds; FV = fair value
  - If SP = FV (an arm's length transaction), recognise any profit/loss immediately
  - If SP < FV, recognise any profit/loss immediately *unless* the apparent loss is compensated by future rentals at below market price, in which case defer and amortise

o If SP > FV, defer the excess over FV and amortise over lease term

Criticism of SSAP 21

- SSAP 21's key usefulness is the enforcing of application of 'commercial substance over legal form'

- Without such enforcement leasing would be an example of off balance sheet financing

- The problem of giving the definition a numerical boundary of 90%: what of the 89% lease?

Hire purchase

- HP agreements exist where the hirer having met all the required instalments can exercise an available purchase option

- The commercial similarity with finance leases means they should be accounted for in the same way

---

Exam focus. A leasing question may be connected to off balance sheet finance in general. In particular, you may be asked to discuss the links between SSAP 21 and FRS 5.

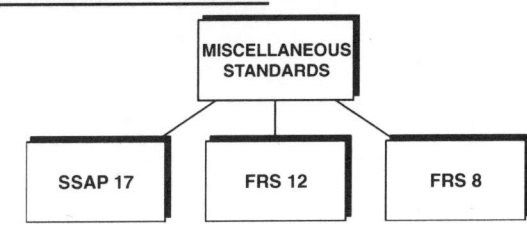

SSAP 17

- *Post balance sheet events (PBSEs)*: events, both favourable and unfavourable, which occur between the balance sheet date and the date on which the financial statements (FS) are approved by the board of directors

- The date on which the financial statements are approved by the board of directors is the date the board of directors formally approves a set of documents as the FS

- There are two types of post balance sheet events:
  - *Adjusting events* are PBSEs which provide additional evidence of conditions existing at the B/S date
  - *Non-adjusting events* are PBSEs which concern conditions which did not exist at the B/S date

Accounting treatment of PBSEs is as follows.

- Financial statements should be prepared on the basis of conditions existing at the B/S date

- *Adjusting PBSE*: amounts included in the financial statements should be changed

- *Non-adjusting PBSE*: disclose if material
  - Nature of the event
  - Estimate of the financial effect (if possible)

- Estimate of the financial effect before taking account of taxation; taxation implications should be explained

- Date on which the FS were approved by the board

- Reversal or maturity of any window-dressing transactions

Window dressing

Refers to the arranging of transactions, the substance of which is primarily to alter the appearance of the balance sheet; not falsification of accounts. SSAP 17 does allow window dressing but full disclosure must be made.

FRS 12

FRS 12 *Provisions, contingent liabilities and contingent assets* was published in September 1998 to remedy some abuses of provisions. It replaced SSAP 18.

- The standard defines a provision as 'a liability of uncertain amount or timing'. Liabilities are 'obligations ... to transfer economic benefits as a result of past transactions or events'

- Entities should not provide for costs that need to be incurred to operate in the future, if those costs could be avoided by the entity's future actions

- The costs of restructuring are to be recognised as a provision only when the entity has an obligation to carry out the restructuring

- The full amount of any decommissioning or environmental liabilities should be recognised from the date on which they arise

- A contingent liability should be disclosed unless the possibility of any outflow of economic benefits to settle it is remote

- A contingent asset should be disclosed where an inflow of economic benefits is probable

The main requirements of the FRS are summarised in the diagram on the next page.

Note. In rare cases it is not clear whether there is a present obligation. In these cases, a past event is deemed to give rise to a present obligation if, taking account of all available evidence, it is more likely than not that a present obligation exists at the balance sheet date.

FRS 8   *11/96*

FRS 8 covers related party disclosures.

Definition: related parties

Two or more parties are related parties when at any time during the financial period:

- One party has direct or indirect control of the other party, *or*

- The parties are subject to common control from the same source, *or*

- One party has influence over the financial and operating policies of the other party to an extent that the other party might be inhibited from pursuing at all times its own separate interests, *or*

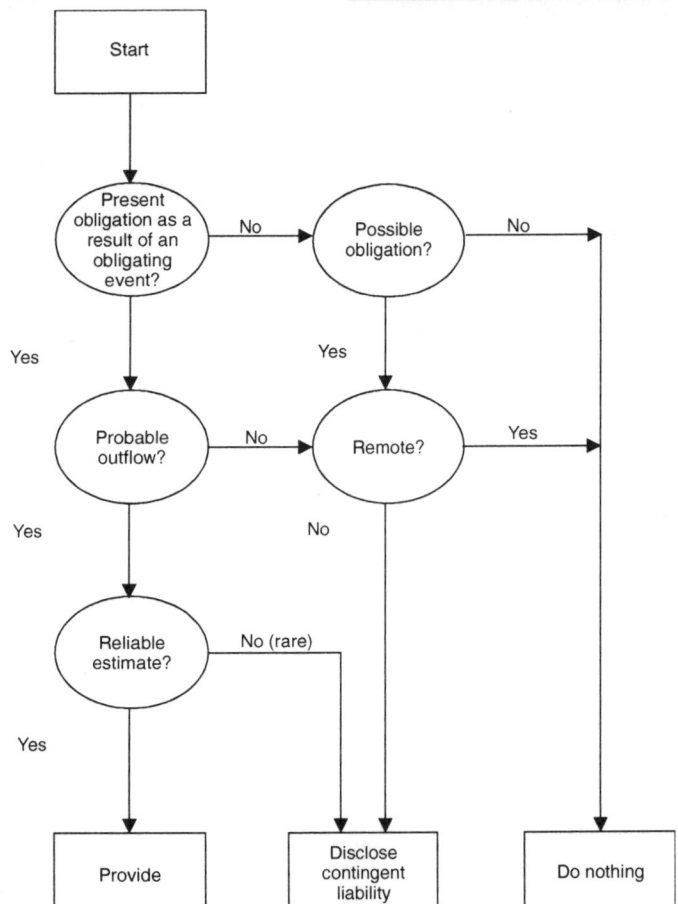

- The parties, in entering a transaction, are subject to influence from the same source to such an extent that one of the parties to the transaction has subordinated its own separate interests

The FRS states that the most important factor in deciding whether two parties are related is the *substance* of their relationship.

'Deemed' and 'presumed' related parties

Examples of related parties are divided into two categories (lists not exhaustive).

- Those where the nature of the relationship is *deemed* to result in the parties being related
  - Ultimate/intermediate parent(s), (fellow) subsidiaries
  - Associates, JVs of itself or any of above
  - Investor/venturer to entity's associate/JV
  - Directors of entity/parent(s), plus immediate family
  - Pension fund of entity or its related parties

- Those where the nature of the relationship is *presumed* to result in the parties being related unless there is evidence to the contrary
  - Key management of entity/parent plus their direct families
  - Owns/controls > 20% voting rights in entity (nominees, direct family, holdings etc)
  - Concert parties exercising control/influence
  - Entity managed by the reporting entity under a management contract

    o Partnerships, companies, trusts, other entities of which directors/people listed above have a controlling interest

Further definitions

- *Control*: the ability to direct the financial and operating policies of an entity with a view to gaining economic benefits from its activities
- *Related party transactions*: the transfer of assets or liabilities or the performance of services by, to or for a related party irrespective of whether a price is charged

Disclosure of transactions and balances

Financial statements should disclose material transactions undertaken with a related party by the entity, irrespective of whether a price is charged, as follows.

- Names of the related parties
- Description of the relationship between the parties
- Description of the transactions
- Amounts involved
- Any other explanations required
- Amounts due to/from related parties at the B/S date
- Amounts w/off related party debts

Disclosure can be on aggregate basis for similar transactions.

Disclosure of control

When the reporting entity is controlled by another party, there should be disclosure of the name of that party and, if different, that of the ultimate controlling party (if not known, that fact should be disclosed). Disclose irrespective of whether any transactions have taken place between the controlling parties and the reporting entity.

Exemptions from disclosure

FRS 8 does *not* require disclosure of the following.

- In consolidated financial statements, of any transactions or balances between group entities that have been eliminated on consolidation

- In a parent's own financial statements when those statements are presented together with its consolidated financial statements

- In the financial statements of > 90% voting subsidiary undertakings, of transactions with entities that are part of the group or investees of the group qualifying as related parties, *if* consolidated a/cs are available (state exemption taken)

- Of pension contributions paid to a pension fund

- Of emoluments in respect of services as an employee of the reporting entity

CA 1985 and the SE require disclosures covering transactions with directors, substantial shareholders and associates.

Exam focus. Part of question 5 in 11/96 asked about sales to a company wholly owned by the selling company's MD.

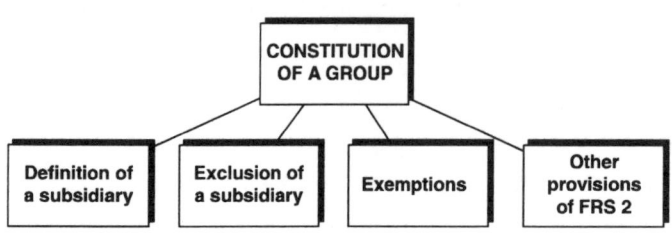

If a company has a subsidiary at its year end, it must prepare group accounts which must be in the form of consolidated accounts.

Definition of a subsidiary   *11/95*

A subsidiary undertaking is one in which the parent:

- Has a majority of the voting rights

- Is a member and can appoint/remove a majority of the board of directors (entitled to the majority of voting rights)

- Is a member and controls alone a majority of the voting rights by agreement with other members

- Has the right to exercise a *dominant influence* through the Memorandum and Articles or a control contract

- Has a *participating interest* and *either*
  - Actually exercises a dominant influence over it, *or*
  - Manages both on a unified basis

Definitions were introduced by FRS 2/CA 1989 to stop the increasing practice of the use of the non-consolidated subsidiary.

- *Control*: the ability of an undertaking to direct the financial and operating policies of another undertaking with a view to gaining economic benefits from its activities

- *Dominant influence*: influence that can be exercised to achieve the operating and financial policies desired by the holder of the influence, notwithstanding the rights or influence of any other party

- *Participating interest*: an interest in shares held for the long term for the purpose of securing a contribution to activities by the exercise of control or influence arising from that interest

- *On a unified basis*: two/+ undertakings are managed on a unified basis if the whole of the operations of the undertakings are integrated and managed as a single unit

- *Held on a long-term basis*: any interest held other than exclusively with a view to subsequent resale

Exclusion of a subsidiary

There may be situations where consolidation would not give a true and fair view of the group's affairs: *exceptional*.

FRS 2

Exclusion from consolidation is *required* by FRS 2 under the following circumstances.

Reason	Accounting treatment
• Severe long-term restrictions hindering exercise of parent's rights	B/S: equity method up to date of severe restrictions less amounts w/off if permanent fall in value
	P&L a/c: dividends received only

- Held exclusively for subsequent resale; has never been consolidated

  Current asset at the lower of cost and net realisable value

- Dissimilar activities *

  Equity method (see Chapter 17)

* Dissimilarity unlikely: could show under SSAP 25.

CA 1985

Exclusion from consolidation is *permitted* under CA 1985 in all of the circumstances cited above, except for dissimilar activities where exclusion is *required*. CA 1985 permits exclusion if the information cannot be obtained without disproportionate expense or undue delay, but this was dismissed as invalid by the ASB.

Exemptions

Where a company has a subsidiary but is itself at least 50% owned by another company established in an EU member state, it is exempt from preparing group accounts subject to the following conditions.

- Intermediate holding company does not have shares or debentures listed on a recognised stock exchange in a member state

- Intermediate holding company is included in the audited consolidated financial statements of a parent undertaking established in the EU

Minority shareholders can request consolidation if they hold > ½ remaining shares in the company or 5% of the total shares.

Also, *small and medium-sized groups* are not required to produce group accounts (unless they are plcs, banks etc) and *cannot* be required to do so by the minority shareholders.

Other provisions of FRS 2

- *Uniform accounting policies* throughout the group: adjust subsidiaries on consolidation; if not possible, make full disclosure of the different policies and the effects

- *Accounting period and dates*: the financial statements of all group companies should be prepared to the same accounting date and for the same accounting period; subsidiaries can prepare 3 months before *if necessary* with appropriate adjustments and disclosure

- *Material purchase of a subsidiary*: disclose sufficient information about the results of the subsidiary acquired to enable shareholders to appreciate its effect

- *Effective date* for acquisitions *and* disposals of a subsidiary should be the date on which control passes

- *Intra group transactions*
    - Profits/losses on any intra group transactions should be eliminated in full
    - Elimination of profit/loss should be set against the interests held by the group *and* the minority interest in respective proportion to their holdings in the relevant undertaking

---

Exam focus. The contents of this chapter are crucial to your understanding of group accounts. You may be asked to judge the status of a group company (subsidiary/associate/investment) and to do so you will need to know all the above definitions and rules. This was the case with question 1 in the 11/95 paper.

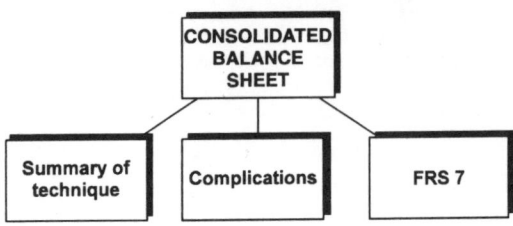

Summary of technique   5/95, 11/96

Consolidated balance sheet

- *Net assets*: always 100% H plus 100% S providing H holds a majority of voting rights

- *Share capital*: H only

- *Reserves*: 100% H plus group share of post-acquisition retained reserves of S less consolidation adjustments

- *Minority interest*: MI share of S's consolidated assets

The method of consolidation is as follows.

- Determine group structure

- Consider adjustments
  - Dividends
  - Provisions for unrealised profits
  - Revaluation to fair value
  - Intercompany stock and cash in transit
  - Intercompany transfer of fixed assets

- Combine net assets, cancelling any intra-group balances
    - Current accounts
    - Proposed dividends of subsidiary
    - Debentures

- Share capital of H only

- *Calculate minority interest in net assets*

MI % of share capital	X
MI % of reserves	X
MI % of revaluations to fair value	X
MI % of unrealised profit	(X)
	X

- *Goodwill*

Cost of investment		X
Assets acquired		
Share capital	X	
Pre-acquisition reserves	X	
Revaluation to fair value	X	
	X	
Group share %		(X)
Goodwill (may be negative)		X

- *FRS 10 treatment*

    - Capitalise and amortise over estimated life through the P & L a/c

    - Capitalise and keep in balance sheet subject to annual impairment review

- *Reserves*

H per question	X
Post-acquisition dividends not yet accounted for	X
Proposed dividends not yet accounted for	(X)
PUP for sales made by H	(X)
	X

S per question	X	
Dividends to be proposed	(X)	
PUP for sales made by S	(X)	
Additional depreciation: transfer of fixed assets	(X)	
Less reserves at acquisition	(X)	
	X	
Group share %		X
		X
Goodwill amortisation		(X)
Consolidated reserves		X

Complications   *5/95, 11/96*

Inter-company transactions

- On consolidation, accounts are prepared as if the group were a single entity and accordingly inter-company transactions need to be cancelled out

- Inter-company accounts may not agree due to items in transit at the year end; push such transactions to their ultimate conclusion

Unrealised profit

Unrealised profit will arise on inter-company transactions where the stock still remains at the B/S date.

- If H sells to S, the unrealised profit lies in H's books

  Debit   Consolidated P&L a/c
  Credit   Group stock (B/S)

- If S sells to H, the unrealised profit lies in S's books and must be shared between H and the MI

  Debit   Consolidated P&L a/c (H's share)
  Debit   Minority interest (MI's share)
  Credit   Group stock (B/S)

Dividend payable by S

- *In S's books*
  Debit   S's reserves
  Credit   Dividend payable

- *In H's books*
  Debit   Dividend receivable
  Credit   H's reserves

On consolidation, cancel the dividend receivable in H's books against dividend payable in S's books leaving dividend payable to the MI in the consol B/S.

Transfer of fixed assets

Likely problems will be:

- Unrealised profit on disposal
- Depreciation charge not based on cost to the group

In exam questions, eliminate the profit from the company that made the profit, and add back the 'excess' depreciation suffered to the reserves of the company that bought the asset.

- *Sale by H*

  o *Profit on disposal*

    Debit   Consolidated P&L a/c
    Credit   Fixed assets

  o *Additional depreciation*

    Debit   Fixed assets
    Credit   Consolidated P&L a/c (H's share)
    Credit   MI (MI's share)

- *Sale by S*

  o *Profit on disposal*

    Debit   Consolidated P&L a/c (H's share)
    Debit   MI (MI's share)
    Credit   Fixed assets

  o *Additional depreciation*

    Debit   Fixed assets
    Credit   Consolidated P&L a/c

Preference shares/debentures

There will be a different % stake taken in these compared to the ordinary share capital. Remember preference shares and debentures give no voting power so they will not be taken account of in control terms; but cancel inter-company dividends/interest etc.

Exam focus. One (but usually several) of these complications will certainly arise in any consolidation question as both the 11/97 and 5/98 papers showed - you must know how to deal with each of them.

FRS 7 *11/96, 5/98*

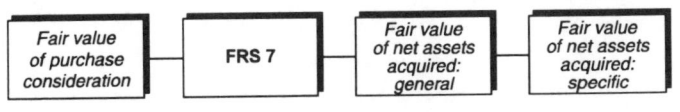

- On consolidation, the *fair value* of the consideration paid for a subsidiary is compared with the *fair value* of its net assets

- *Fair value:* the amount for which an asset (liability) could be exchanged in an arm's length transaction

Fair value of purchase consideration

Main (likely) components of purchase consideration:

- *Ordinary shares*
  - If quoted, the market price on the date of acquisition
  - If no suitable market price exists, then estimate
    - Value of similar quoted securities
    - PV of the future cash flows of instrument issued
    - Any cash alternative which was offered

- *Other securities:* base value on similar principles

- *Cash or monetary assets:* amounts paid or payable

- *Non-monetary assets:* market price, estimated realisable values, independent valuations or other evidence

- *Deferred consideration:* discount amounts after calculation on above principles; appropriate discount rate is that at which the acquirer could obtain a similar borrowing

- *Contingent consideration*: use probable amount; when the actual amount is known, record in consolidated financial statements and adjust consolidated goodwill

Acquisition costs should be included in the cost of the investment. No internal costs may be capitalised, nor costs of issuing capital instruments.

Fair value of net assets acquired: general

- *Identifiable net assets*
  - Identifiable assets and liabilities acquired should be those of the acquired entity at *the date of acquisition*
  - Should *not* reflect increases or decreases resulting from the acquirer's intentions for future actions
  - The assets and liabilities should be identified and valued using the acquirer's accounting policies

- *Non-monetary assets*: FV = the lower of replacement cost and recoverable amount

- *Monetary items*: FV = the amount of money payable/ receivable; long-term payables/receivables which do not bear interest at current market rates should be discounted to PV

- *Future losses and reorganisation costs*: FRS 7 does not allow *any* provision to be made for either future losses or reorganisation costs as they are *not liabilities* of the acquired entity at the date of acquisition

- *Business held for resale*: if part of the acquired company is to be resold then the individual assets and liabilities of that part should be excluded from the FV exercise and included as a current asset investment at NRV (must have purchaser; disposal to occur < 1 year after acquisition)

- *Investigation period and goodwill adjustment*: FV exercise based upon conditions existing at the date of acquisition but may be time consuming; time limit = date the acquirer's first post-acquisition FS approved by the directors, otherwise estimate; adjust in the next FS; thereafter recognise as post-acquisition gains and losses

Fair value of net assets acquired: specific

- *Tangible fixed assets*
  - Market value
  - Depreciated replacement cost

- *Intangible fixed assets:* replacement cost, normally estimated market value

- *Stocks and WIP*
  - If stocks traded on market use current market prices
  - Other stocks, WIP: value at lower of replacement cost and NRV

- *Monetary assets and liabilities:* as noted above.

Multi-company structures

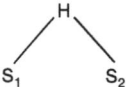

In the consolidated B/S:

- A single figure is given for MI

- Separate totals for goodwill and capital reserves arising (if goodwill capitalised and amortised)

Sub-subsidiaries   *11/95, 5/98*

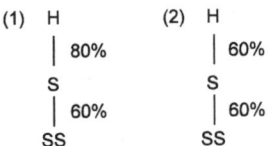

H must prepare group accounts in respect of each subsidiary it controls whether directly or indirectly.

- In (1) H *controls* S; S *controls* SS therefore H *controls* SS

- In (2) H *owns* 60% of S; S *owns* 60% of SS, H effectively *owns* SS

Direct (single-stage) method of consolidation

Where any sub-subsidiaries are brought directly into H's books:

- *Net assets*: show what group *controls*

- *Capital and reserves*: based on *effective holdings*, eg 80% × 80% = 64%

Use this method in the exam - it is quick.

Indirect (two-stage) method of consolidation

S prepares consolidated accounts, which are then brought into H's consolidated accounts; often used in practice.

Exam focus. The May 98 paper had a complex consolidation question involving a sub-subsidiary. Easy marks are available if you couldn't handle the more complicated calculations.

Date of effective control

The general rule for the date on which the sub-subsidiary comes under the control of the holding company is, either:

- Date S acquired if S already holds shares in SS, or
- If S acquires SS later, that later date

'D' shaped groups

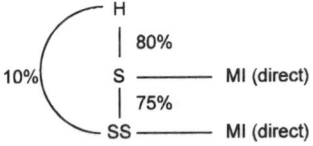

In practice several consolidations might be carried out, using procedures which are the same as in the indirect method of consolidation for subsidiaries.

- S with SS
- H with the S group
- H with SS (for the direct holding of 10%)

In an examination, however, the single stage is recommended to save time. In the structure above there is:

- A *direct* minority in S of		20%
- A *direct* minority in SS of	15%	
- An *indirect* minority in SS of 20% × 75%	15%	
		30%

Now proceed as for a typical sub-subsidiary situation by the direct (single stage) method.

Exam focus. You can check that you have worked out the correct minority interests by assuming a dividend distribution of £100 from SS. In the above situation:

S will receive £75	
H will receive 80% × £75	60
H will receive 10% × £100	10
	70
Leaving for MI in SS	30

Basic principles   *11/95*

Adjustments required for consolidation of a subsidiary:

- Eliminate intra-group sales and purchases

- Eliminate any unrealised profits on intra-group purchases still in stock at the year end

- Eliminate any intra-group dividends received and paid - show only H's dividends

- Show MI as a separate line after PAT

- Include group share of any extraordinary items in the subsidiary's accounts where material in a group context

For inclusion of subsidiary:

- Combine all H and S results from turnover to PAT (where acquisition is mid-year, use time apportioned basis)

- Exclude any investment income that is intra-group

- Calculate MI

   ○ Where there are no preference shares, MI = % × PAT

   ○ Where there are preference shares, an additional working is required

Pre-acquisition dividends

Two ways to calculate pre-acquisition element of a dividend.

- To the extent that post-acquisition profits are insufficient to cover the dividend, the distribution must be out of pre-acquisition profits; more commonly done in practice, *or*

- Apportion the dividend on a time basis between the pre- and post-acquisition periods, so only post-acquisition dividends are be taken to H's reserves (recommended)

   o Pre-acquisition dividend: *Debit* Dividend receivable/cash, *Credit* Cost of investment

   o Post-acquisition dividend: *Debit* Dividend receivable/cash, *Credit* P & L a/c

---

Exam focus. Expect a consolidated P&L with an associate, given FRS 9 is relatively new (see Chapter 17).

Form and content

To show the results of the group for an accounting period as if it were a single entity.

- *Turnover to profit after tax (PAT)*: 100% H + 100% S (excluding dividend receivable from subsidiary and adjustments for inter-company transactions)

- *Inter-company sales*: strip out inter-company activity from both turnover and cost of sales:

   o *Goods sold by H*: increase cost of sales by unrealised profit

   o *Goods sold by S*: increase cost of sales by full amount of unrealised profit and decrease MI by their share of unrealised profit

- *Depreciation*
    - If the value of S's fixed assets have been subjected to a fair value uplift then any additional depreciation must be charged in the consolidated P&L a/c
    - MI will need to be adjusted for their share

- *Transfer of fixed assets*: expenses must be increased by any profit on the transfer and reduced by any additional depreciation on the increased carrying value of the asset

- *Minority interest*

S's profit after tax (PAT)		X
Less:	*unrealised profit	(X)
	*profit on disposal of fixed assets	(X)
	additional depreciation following FV uplift	(X)
Add:	** additional depreciation following disposal of fixed assets	X
		X
		X
MI%		X

* Only applicable if sales of goods and fixed assets made by subsidiary

** Only applicable if sale of fixed assets made by holding company

- *Dividends*: H's only *because*
    - S's dividend is due (i) to H; and (ii) to MI
    - *H has taken in its share by including the results of S in* the consolidated P&L a/c; MI have taken their share by being given a proportion of S's PAT (PAT = dividends + retained profit)

- *Retained reserves*: as per B/S calculations

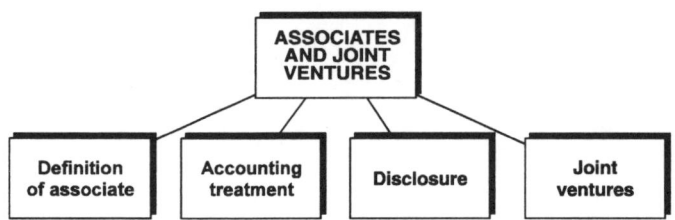

Companies often conduct business through other companies in which they have a substantial but not a controlling interest. Not sufficient to disclose dividend income etc; affects EPS and the P/E ratio.

Definition of associate   *5/95, 11/95*

Associates

FRS 9: an associate exists where:

- Investor holds a *participating interest*
- Investor exercises *significant influence*

Participating interest

An interest held in the share of another entity on a long-term basis for the purpose of securing a contribution to the investor's activities by the exercise of control or influence arising from or related to that interest.

Significant influence

This essentially involves participation in the financial and operating policy decisions (including dividend policy). Representation on the board is indicative but not conclusive.

Presumptions

- If ≥ 20% or more of equity voting rights, presumption of significant influence unless clearly demonstrated otherwise

- If < 20% of equity voting rights, presumption of no significant influence unless clearly demonstrated otherwise

In applying the above test, holdings of the parent company and subsidiaries should be aggregated but holdings via another associated company should be excluded.

Accounting treatment

Consolidated balance sheet

Associated undertakings should be accounted for under the equity method of accounting

- Interest in associated undertaking

Investing group's share of net assets other than goodwill of the associate (after attributing FVs to net assets at time of acquisition)	X
Investing group's share of any goodwill in the associate financial statements	X
Premium paid (or discount) on the acquisition insofar as it has not already been written off or amortised	X/(X)
Investment in associated company	X

- Additional disclosures are required where the investor's share exceeds 15% of the gross assets, liabilities or operating result of the investing group
  - Turnover
  - Fixed assets

o Current assets

o Current liabilities (< 1 year and > 1 year)

If the investor's share exceeds 25% of gross assets etc, the investor's share of the following must be shown

o Turnover

o Profit before tax

o Tax

o Profit after tax

o Fixed assets

o Current assets

o Liabilities < 1 year

o Liabilities > 1 year

Consolidated P&L

- Group share of associate's operating results immediately after group operating profit

- Amortisation of goodwill (if any)

- Group share of associate's profit before tax included within the amounts for the group

- Group share of tax charge of associate disclosed separately within the group tax charge

Disclosure

- *Interest in associates*: names of principal associated companies and:

  o Proportion of issued shares held by the investing group

  o Accounting period if different from investor's

  o Indication of the nature of their businesses

- *Retained profit*: group share of the aggregate *net profit less losses retained* by associates

- *Group reserves*: group share of the *post acquisition accumulated reserves* of associates and any movement

Benefits and weaknesses of equity accounting

- *Benefits*
  - Where there is significant influence, showing just dividends received may not give indication of underlying contribution by the associate.
  - Major holders with influence may dictate dividend policy, taking growth in value of underlying assets, not income
  - Without dominant influence it is still unsuitable to acquisition account

- *Weakness*: using the equity method (vs acquisition accounting) may be useful for the creative accountant where the 'subsidiary' has a high level of borrowing

Joint ventures

FRS 9: a joint venture is an entity in which the reporting entity holds an interest on a long-term basis and is *jointly controlled* by the reporting entity and one or more other ventures under a contractual arrangement.

Joint control

A reporting entity jointly controls a venture with one or more other entities if none of the entities alone can control that entity but all together can do so and decisions on financial and operating policy essential to the activities, economic performance and financial position of that venture require each venturer's concern.

Accounting treatment

Joint ventures are included in consolidated financial statements using the *gross equity method*, ie like associates but

- In consolidated P&L joint ventures turnover should not be shown as part of the group turnover

- In consolidated B/S group share of gross assets and liabilities underlying the net equity amount should be shown as amplification of the net amount

- Except for profit before tax in the P&L, any supplementary information given for joint ventures, either in the P&L or B/S must be shown clearly separate from accounts for the group and must not be included in group total

Disclosures

As for associates

Joint arrangements

Participants in a joint arrangement that is not an entity (ie not a subsidiary, joint venture or associate) should account for their own assets, liabilities and cash flows measured according to the terms of the agreement governing the arrangement.

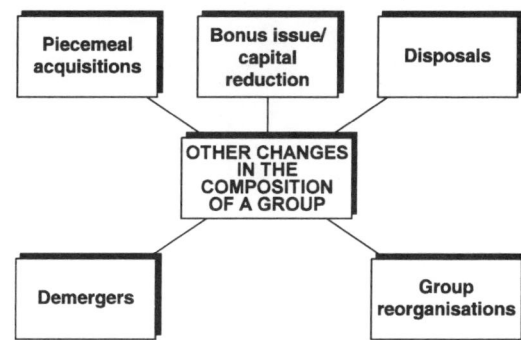

Piecemeal acquisitions

11/95

Acquisitions may not take place all at once; a controlling interest may be built up over a period of time. There are two possible ways of dealing with the subsidiary in the consolidated accounts.

- Only take account of the subsidiary when control is achieved (per FRS 2)

- If the company has already been equity accounted for when it was an associate, then account for additional interest separately (step-by-step method)

Suggested method

The decisive factor is whether or not there is an intention when a minority holding of shares is bought, to acquire control ultimately. A rule-of-thumb to piecemeal acquisitions:

- Ignore share purchases which keep equity share < 20%; make no step-by-step method calculations before the bought company becomes an associate

- When the purchase of shares first takes a company's holding > 20% (up to 50%), treat all shares purchased up to this date as a single block of purchases for the calculation of pre-acquisition profits

- For future (significant) purchases up to the time when control is eventually acquired, the step-by-step method should be applied

Exam focus. Question 1 of the 11/95 paper included the piecemeal acquisition of a sub-subsidiary.

Bonus issue/capital reduction

Bonus issue

- There is no alteration in percentage holding of any party

- Goodwill calculation: ignore the effect of the bonus issue, so use reserves and share capital as they stood at acquisition

Capital reduction

This involves the reduction in nominal value of shares. We are using calculations which show net assets (pre-acquisition reserves and share capital), so any change in NV of shares at a later date is ignored.

Disposals   *11/97*

Calculation of gains or loss

- *In holding company*

Sale proceeds	X
Less cost of investment	(X)
Profit/(loss): taxable	X/(X)

- *In group accounts*

  Either

Sale proceeds		X
Less: net assets now disposed of	X	
goodwill not yet w/off through P&L a/c	X	
		X
Profit/(loss)		X/(X)

  Or

Profit/(loss) per holding company	X
Less post acquisition retained reserves now disposed of	(X)
	X
Add goodwill previously written off through P&L a/c	X
	X

FRS 2: goodwill on acquisition which has not passed through the P&L a/c by amortisation must be included as part of profit/loss on disposal; so any goodwill written off directly against reserves when it arose will have to be reinstated and taken into account in the disposal calculations.

Full disposal

- *Treatment in P&L a/c*
  - Consolidate results to date of disposal

- o Show group gain or loss as *exceptional item* after operating profit and before interest

- *Treatment in B/S*: no MI and no consolidation as there is no subsidiary at the year end

Partial disposals

- *Subsidiary to subsidiary*
  - o MI in P&L a/c will be based on % before and after disposal ie time apportion
  - o MI in B/S is based on year end %

- *Subsidiary to associate*
  - o *P&L a/c*
    - – Treat as subsidiary to date of disposal; consolidate for correct number of months and show MI for that amount
    - – Treat as associate thereafter
  - o *B/S:* equity valuation based on y/e holding

- *Subsidiary to trade investment*
  - o *P&L a/c*
    - – Treat as subsidiary to date of disposal
    - – Show dividend income only thereafter
  - o *B/S*: leave investment valued at equity valuation at date of disposal but consider if write-down required

Dividends

The retained reserves/net assets at the date of disposal of the subsidiary are calculated deducting *only* dividends to which the holding company is entitled, ie dividends paid up to the date of disposal and dividends proposed if shares sold ex-div.

Pro-forma calculation at the date of disposal:

Retained profits brought forward	X
Profit after tax and extraordinary items to date of disposal	X
Dividends paid/proposed at date of disposal	(X)
	X

Disclosure

- *Results for the year*: for any material disposals, give significant information to enable the shareholders to appreciate the effect on consolidated results

- *FRS 3* requires the results of discontinued operations to be analysed separately

- Disclose in respect of each material disposal of a previously acquired business or business segment
  - The profit or loss on the disposal
  - The amount of purchased goodwill attributable to a disposal and how it has been treated in determining the profit/loss on disposal
  - The accounting treatment adopted and the amount of the proceeds, in situations where no profit/loss is recorded on a disposal because the proceeds were accounted for as a reduction in cost of the acquisition

---

Exam focus. In 11/97 you were asked to prepare the consolidated profit and loss account of a group which had disposed of a subsidiary.

Group reorganisations

Why groups change internal structure

- May desire to float a business to reduce gearing of group: the holding company needs initially to transfer the business into a separate company

- May transfer companies to another business during a divisionalisation process

- Business may desire a quotation on the stock market: may reverse the group into another company with a quotation

- Efficiencies of group structure for tax

Provided there is no change in MI % holding there will be no impact on the consolidated financial statements, although change in the individual companies will be major eg profit/loss recorded in books, acquisition in buyer's books.

New top holding company (eg for flotation vehicle)

Merger accounting allowed by FRS 6 (see Chapter 19) in this situation.

Subsidiary moved up

For selling off one subsidiary, or to split diverse business.

- S_1 could transfer its investment in S_2 to H as a dividend *in specie* (paid other than cash) or by H paying cash; a share for share exchange is not possible because an allotment by H to S_1 is void

- S_1 must have sufficient distributable profits for a dividend *in specie*; if the investment in S_2 has been revalued then that can be treated as a realised profit for the purposes of determining the legality of the distribution

- H must write down investment in S_1, but no other accounting rules exist here

- A transfer for cash is probably easiest, but there are still legal pitfalls as to what is distributable, depending on how the transfer is recorded

- No effect on the group financial statements as the group has stayed the same: has made no acquisition or disposal

Subsidiary moved along

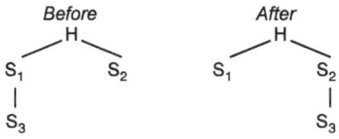

The problem of an effective distribution does not arise here because H did not buy the subsidiary. There may be problems with financial assistance if S_2 pays less than the fair value to purchase S_3 as a prelude to S_1 leaving the group.

Subsidiary moved down

This situation could arise if H is foreign and S_1 and S_2 are UK companies; can form a UK tax group.

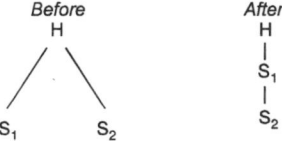

If S_1 paid cash for S_2, the transaction would be straightforward (as described above). The law is again unclear on the issue of whether H should recognise a gain on the sale if S_2 is sold for more or less than carrying value.

Demergers

A demerger will usually involve splitting up an existing group into two or more separate groups.

Reasons

- Diversification leads to stretching of management resources

- Demerger brings back focus for management

- Can improve P/E rating because of this

- Prevent takeover bid

Methods

- H transfers shares in S to its shareholders as a dividend *in specie*

- H transfers a *trade* to another company S, often formed for the purpose, and in exchange S issues shares to H's shareholders

- H transfers shares in S1 to another company S2, which in return issues shares to the shareholders in H; the transaction will always involve a distribution by H to its shareholders

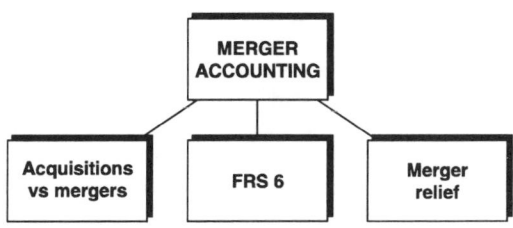

Acquisitions vs mergers

There are two types of business combination.

- One company takes over the business of another company for its own benefit by buying out the previous shareholders

- Two companies combine their resources for mutual benefit; there is continuity of ownership via a share for share exchange

Traditional acquisition accounting is not considered appropriate in the second situation.

Differences between acquisition and merger accounting

In books of H	*Acquisition method*	*Merger method*
Investment in S	Record at FV of consideration given (including premium)	Record at NV of shares issued and FV of other consideration
On consolidation		
Net assets of S	Revalue to FV at date of acquisition	Assets of both companies remain at book values

	Acquisition method	*Merger method*
Goodwill	Goodwill arises: dealt with under SSAP 22	No goodwill arises but there may be 'differences on consolidation' (see below)
Pre-acquisition reserves	Not consolidated; frozen out	All reserves are 'pooled'
Comparatives	Not restated: only post-acquisition results recognised	Restated on a combined basis: effect of merger applied retrospectively

Differences on consolidation: merger method

A	£	B	£
Carrying value of investment (= NV of shares issued + FV of other consideration)	X	Nominal value of shares acquired	X

- If A > B (debit balance): treat as an effective 'capitalisation' of reserves, ie debit to consolidated reserves

- If A < B (credit balance): treat as (capital) reserve arising on consolidation

FRS 6

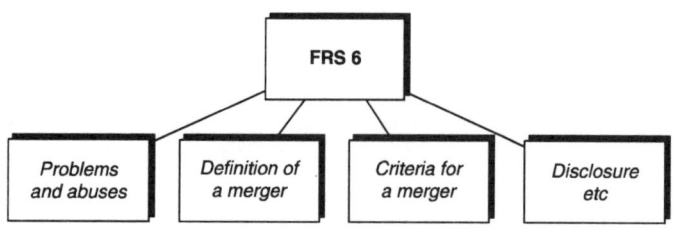

Problems and abuses

- Two methods leads to lack of comparability
- True mergers are difficult to define
- Acquisition accounting *can* account for all combinations
- The merger method is not used much in practice
- There is little overseas support

FRS 6 was introduced to restrict merger accounting to genuine mergers.

Definition of a merger

FRS 6 defines a merger as a business combination resulting in:

- A new reporting entity
- Shareholders of the entities form a fairly equal partnership
- Mutual sharing of risks and benefits
- No dominant party for whatever reason

Criteria for a merger

FRS 6 sets out the following criteria.

- No party to the combination is portrayed as either acquirer or acquired

- All parties to the combination participate in establishing the management structure of the combined entity (not necessarily equal management participation)

- The relative size of the combining entities is not so disparate that one party dominates the combined entity by virtue of its size

- No more than an immaterial proportion of the FV of consideration received is represented by non-equity consideration

- No equity shareholders of any of the combining entities retain any material interest in the future performance of only part of the combined entity

In addition, CA 1985 criteria *must* be met if merger accounting is used.

- $\geq$ 90% of the NV of the relevant shares in the undertaking acquired must be held by the group

- Must be achieved as a result of an arrangement providing for the issue of *equity shares* by the parent company

- The *FV* of any consideration other than equity shares $\leq$ *10% NV* of the equity shares issued

Disclosure etc

The disclosure requirements for both merger accounting and acquisition accounting under FRS 6 are both comprehensive and detailed.

Exam focus. Assume in an exam that everything which seems sensible should be disclosed!

FRS 6 contains some additional material.

- Merger accounting is allowed in some *group reconstructions* and in some combinations involving a *new parent company*; it is the *overall spirit* of the transaction which indicates the treatment

- *Merger expenses* should be charged to the P&L a/c of the combined entity at the date of merger, *not* as a movement on reserves, per FRS 3

- *Substantial acquisitions* require additional disclosures

- *Differences* in NV of shares issued vs NV of shares received etc is a movement on reserves

- *Existing* balances on 'new' subsidiary's share premium or capital redemption reserve are movements on reserves

The last two items should be shown in the reconciliation of movements in shareholders' funds.

Merger relief

S 131 CA 1985: where an issuing company has secured ≥ 90% equity holding in another company in an arrangement involving the issue of its own equity shares, s 130 CA 1985 (requirement to create share premium a/c) does not apply.

- Call difference between NV and market value a *merger relief reserve* or record shares issued at NV only

- S 131 only applies to issue of shares taking investment over the 90% threshold

---

Exam focus. FRS 6 has yet to appear in an exam question.

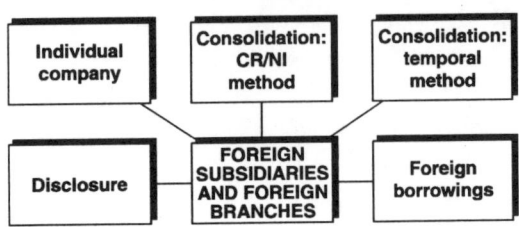

SSAP 20 aim: to produce results which are generally compatible with the effects of rate changes on a company's cash flows and its equity; to ensure that the financial statements present a true and fair view of the results of management actions.

Conversion vs translation

- *Conversion*: physical exchange of currencies

- *Translation*: expression of one currency in the value of the other

Individual company

During the period

- Translate each transaction at *exchange rate on date of transaction* (Average Rate (AR) for a period may be used as an approximation, if rates do not fluctuate significantly)

- Where transaction is to be settled at contracted rate, use *contracted rate*

- Where a *trading* transaction is covered by related or matching *forward contract*, the forward rate *may* be used

Where the transaction is settled during the period the exchange difference arising is a realised gain or loss and is reported in the P&L a/c for the year.

At the balance sheet date

- *Non-monetary* assets (eg fixed assets, stock): do not restate (ie they remain at historical rate (HR))

- *Monetary* assets and liabilities (including long-term items): restate at closing rate (CR) (or contract rate/forward rate)

Treatment of exchange differences

Part of profit/loss for the year on ordinary activities.

- On *trading transactions*: under 'other operating income or charges'

- On *financing transactions*: under 'other interest receivable/payable and similar income/charges'

Consolidation: CR/NI method   5/96

The method of translation used should reflect the financial and other operational relationships which exist between an investing company and its foreign enterprises. The main factor which determines the method to be used is the degree of dependence of the foreign enterprise on the economic environment of the investing company's currency.

The *closing rate/net investment method* recognises that the investment of a company is in the net worth of the foreign enterprise rather than a direct investment in its individual assets and liabilities. *Problem*: criteria for using this method are not clear cut.

Exchange rates

- B/S
  - All assets and liabilities @ CR
  - Within shareholders' funds (for exam purposes)

- – Share capital and pre-acquisition reserves @ HR
- – Post acquisition reserves: balancing figure

- *P&L a/c:* all items at *either* CR *or* AR, once selected must be applied consistently, except dividend @ actual rate

Exchange differences

Exchange differences arising on the retranslation of a company's net investment in its foreign enterprise should be dealt with as *adjustments to reserves.*

Differences may result from factors unrelated to the trading performance or financing of the foreign enterprise: in particular they do not represent or measure changes in actual or prospective cash flows. If they were taken to the P&L a/c the results from trading operations would be distorted.

Calculation of exchange differences re subsidiary/associate

	£
Closing NA @ CR	X
Less opening NA @ OR	X
	X
Less retained profit per translated P&L	X
Exchange differences	X/(X)
Group share (%)	X/(X)

Show as a movement on reserves.

Exam focus. Question 1 in 5/96 asked you to determine the appropriate method to use in a given situation. You were then required to translate the subsidiary's P&L a/c, prepare the consolidated P&L a/c and prepare a statement reconciling opening and closing consolidated reserves.

Consolidation: temporal method 11/98

Where the affairs of a foreign enterprise are so closely interlinked with those of the investing company that its results may be regarded as being more dependent on the economic environment of the investing company's currency than its own reporting currency, it should be included in the consolidated financial statements as if the transactions had been entered into by the investing company in its own currency.

Factors to be considered

- Extent to which the cash flows of the enterprise have a direct impact upon those of the investing company

- Extent to which the functioning of the enterprise is directly dependent upon the investing company

- Currency in which the majority of the trading transactions are denominated

- Major currency to which the operation is exposed in its financing structure

Situations where temporal method appropriate

Where the foreign enterprise:

- Acts as a selling agent receiving stocks of goods from the investing company and remitting the proceeds back

- Produces raw materials/manufactures parts which are then shipped to the investing company for inclusion in its own products

- Is located overseas for tax, exchange control or similar reasons to act as a means of raising finance for other companies in the group

Exchange rates

Same as individual financial statement rules.

- *Balance sheet*

FA	@ HR
Stocks	@ HR
Monetary assets and liabilities	@ CR
Shareholders' funds	
Share capital and pre-acquisition reserves	@ HR
Post-acquisition reserves	Balancing figure

- *P&L a/c*

Depreciation	@ HR
Opening stocks	@ HR
Closing stocks	@ HR
Sales, purchases and other expenses	@ Avg rate
Dividends	@ Actual rate

Exchange differences

The exchange difference is treated as for the individual company situation. The exchange difference arising on *retranslation* is reported as part of the profit or loss on ordinary activities. The exchange difference represents the settlement differences arising during the year *and* the retranslation of the subsidiary's opening monetary items.

> *Exam focus.* In exams the exchange difference is arrived at by calculating the retained profit for the foreign enterprise in sterling terms and working back to get the exchange difference as a balancing figure.

Foreign borrowings

Individual financial statements

Where *foreign currency borrowings* have been used to finance/hedge *foreign equity investments*:

- The foreign equity investments *may* be translated at the closing rate; exchange differences taken to reserves: *but* large numbers can be hidden away; partly overcome by greater prominence in statement of recognised gains and losses

- Exchange differences on the foreign currency borrowings should then be offset against this reserve movement

- *Conditions for offset*
  - Offset restricted to the differences on the foreign equity investments
  - Foreign currency borrowings should not exceed the total cash that the investments are expected to be able to generate, whether from profits or otherwise
  - Treatment adopted must be consistently applied

Consolidated financial statements

- Where foreign currency borrowings have been used to finance/hedge foreign group equity investments, exchange differences on such borrowings *may* be offset as reserve movements against the exchange differences on the retranslation of the net investments in foreign enterprises

- Conditions are as above *plus*: the relationship must justify the use of the *closing rate method*

- Under the *temporal method*, as all exchange differences are taken to the P&L a/c, any exchange differences on related borrowings should also be taken to the P&L a/c

Disclosure

- *Accounting policy note:* method used in the translation of the financial statements of foreign enterprises; treatment of exchange differences

- *Gains/losses:* net amount of exchange gains and losses on foreign currency borrowing less deposits

- *Movements on reserves:* net movement on reserves arising from exchange differences

- *Gains on long-term monetary items: unrealised profit:* under SSAP 20, exchange gains arising on long-term (> 1 year) monetary items are deemed to be 'unrealised'

  o Where there are doubts as to the convertibility of a currency, consider if prudent to restrict the amount of the gain to be recognised in the P&L a/c

  o Where gains on long-term monetary items are included in the P&L a/c, this represents a departure from CA 1985 and a note is required, covering *particulars, reasons* and *effect* of the departure

---

Exam focus. Consolidation of a foreign subsidiary came up in November 98. You had to justify the choice of method of translation and prepare a working schedule for a consolidated balance sheet.

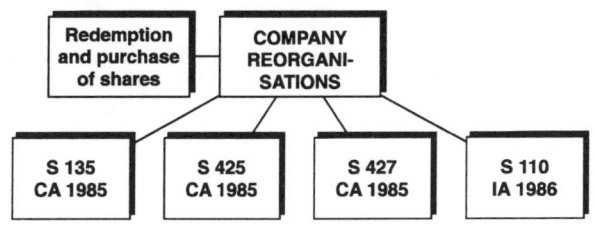

Redemption and purchase of shares 5/97

Advantages (in particular of 'purchase')

- *For unquoted companies*
    - Increase marketability of shares (co as buyer)
    - Retention of family control (on death/retirement)
    - Aid employee share schemes (marketability)
    - Attract new capital (marketability)

- *For all companies*
    - Use for surplus funds
    - Greater flexibility in ordering capital structure

Legal formalities

- Authorised by Articles

- Non-redeemable shares in issue after redemption/ purchase

- Shares must be fully paid

- In general, shares must be redeemed/purchased either out of distributable profits or proceeds of fresh issue

- *For purchase of shares only*
  - o *Off market purchase*: contract must be approved by special resolution prior to purchase
  - o *Market purchase*: ordinary resolution or limited general authority

Maintenance of capital

Protection of the buffer fund (share capital + non-distributable reserves):

- Redemption/purchase out of profits s 170(1): transfer to CRR = NV of shares redeemed/purchased

- Redemption/purchase wholly/partly out of proceeds of fresh issue s 170(2): transfer to CRR = NV of shares redeemed/purchased less proceeds of issue

Premium on redemption/purchase

- *Normal rule s 160(1)*: any premium on redemption must be paid out of distributable profits; ie charge premium to distributable profits, *Debit* P&L a/c, *Credit* Cash

- *Exception to normal rule s 160(2)*: Charge premium to share premium account up to the *lowest of*
  - o Proceeds of fresh issue
  - o Premium on the *original* issue of shares being redeemed/purchased
  - o Balance on share premium account (including any premium arising on the fresh issue)
  - o Premium on redemption

Redemption/purchase out of capital

Private companies *only* can use capital.

- *Legal formalities*

  - Authorised by Articles
  - Must use distributable profits/fresh issue first
  - Special resolution
  - Statutory declaration of solvency
  - Auditors' report on statutory declaration
  - Publicity

- Reduction in buffer fund = 'permissible capital payment' (PCP), calculated as follows.

Purchase price of shares redeemed/purchased		X
Less: available distributable profits	X	
proceeds of fresh issue (if any)	X	
		(X)
Permissible capital payment (PCP)		X

- *Accounting entries*

  S 171(4) & (5): amend previous calculation to: NV of shares redeemed less (proceeds of new issue *and* PCP)

  - If answer +ve then transfer this amount to CRR
  - If −ve debit amount to share premium, share capital or any non-distributable reserve

S 135 Reduction of share capital   5/97

Legal formalities

- Authorised by articles
- Special resolution
- Court sanction

Purposes

- Extinguish uncalled liability on share capital *
- Cancel share capital unrepresented by available assets
- Pay off share capital in excess of company's wants *

* S 136 requires: that a list of creditors must be drawn up; they must either consent to the scheme or be provided for to the court's satisfaction.

> *Exam focus.* Capital reorganisation was examined for the first time in May 1997.

S 425 Internal reconstruction

This is whenever creditors are involved in the scheme.

Legal formalities

- Majority in number and 75% in value of each class of creditor and member affected must approve
- Court may then sanction it
- All creditors and members then bound by the scheme

Procedure

- Open reorganisation account
- Transfer in all shares/debentures to be replaced
- Put all asset write downs/revaluations and expenses of scheme through this account
- Issue new shares/debentures from this account
- Transfer balance of account to a capital reserve (or write off against eg share premium account if a debit balance)

S 127: Protection of parties to the scheme

Holders of ≥ 15% in aggregate of the class of shares in question may apply to the court to have the variation cancelled. The decision of the court is final.

S 427 External reconstruction

Legal formalities

When there is a 'reconstruction' into a newly formed company, then may by court order:

- Transfer the undertaking to the newly formed company
- Allot shares/debentures in new company
- Dissolve old company without a formal winding up

Procedure

Close off ledger accounts in books of old company. Open up ledger accounts in books of new company, as follows.

- *Open realisation a/c*: transfer all assets and liabilities to be taken over by new company at book value

- *Open sundry members a/c* (columns for ordinary and preference shareholders): transfer share capital, P&L balances, assets w/off or losses, gains on realisation

- *Purchase consideration to members*
  - *Credit* realisation a/c
  - *Debit* sundry member a/c
  - Any profit/loss on realisation: to sundry members a/c (ordinary)

- *In new company*: open up *purchase of business a/c*
  - *Credit* with assets taken over (*Debit* asset a/cs)

- o   *Debit* with liabilities taken over (*Credit* liabilities a/cs)
- o   *Debit* with purchase consideration (*Credit* shares, debentures etc)

Any balance = reserve/goodwill

S 110 Insolvency Act 1986

In voluntary liquidations the liquidator may transfer the assets of the company to a new company in exchange for shares in the new company. Under s 110 the old company can retain certain assets eg cash and make a distribution to shareholders.

- ● *Advantages*
  - o   Court sanction not required
  - o   Scheme approved by special resolution

- ● *Disadvantages*
  - o   Dissenting shareholder can serve notice on liquidator preventing scheme, and require the purchase of their shares at price to be agreed or set by arbitration
  - o   Less flexible than ss 425/427 with no varying of class rights

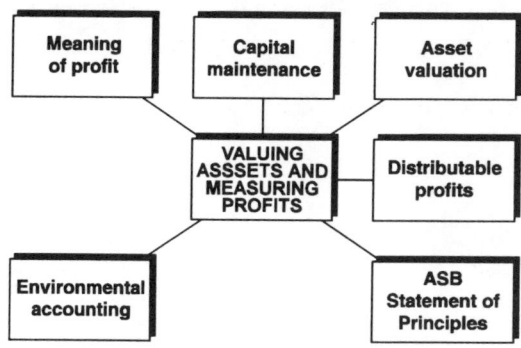

Meaning of profit

Sandilands Committee (after Hicks' economist's view of profit/ income): 'a company's profit for the year is the maximum value which the company can distribute during the year, and still expect to be as well off as at the end of the year as it was at the beginning'.

Balance sheet is the primary accounting statement.

Capital maintenance

There are different views of capital maintenance.

Financial capital maintenance

Under historical cost accounting (HCA), amount maintained is the capital sum put into the business by the owner.

Focusing on the equity ownership of the company is often referred to as the *proprietary concept of capital*: if we pay all profits out as dividends and inflation exists then in future our business will gradually run down, as our cash will become insufficient to buy replacement stock.

Operating capital maintenance

Capital is looked at as the capacity to maintain a level of assets, alternatively referred to as the *physical capacity capital maintenance concept*, or the *entity concept*: by using replacement cost for our cost of sales we will set aside enough cash to buy replacement assets.

Asset valuation   5/98

Entry and exit values are examples of current value accounting which attempt to find an alternative accounting convention which combines the advantages of objective reporting with the use of realistic values for assets.

Entry values

Non-monetary assets are converted to current replacement cost.

- *Advantages*
    - Ensures operating capital maintenance by recognising operating profit
    - Separates operational from holding gains, so can distinguish gains under the control of management
    - Realistic value of capital employed

- *Disadvantages*
    - Based upon historic convention
    - Replacement costs may not always be available
    - Subjective

Exit values

Income = closing capital valued at exit price less opening capital at exit price; where exit prices are the amount at which non-monetary assets could be sold in an orderly realisation.

● *Advantages*

  ○ Based on the concept of opportunity cost

  ○ Most people understand realisable values

  ○ Shows creditors amounts available on a winding up

● *Disadvantages*

  ○ Not based upon going concern concept

  ○ Valuation of assets is subjective

  ○ Assumption of orderly realisation of assets in their existing state may be misleading

  ○ Does not ensure operating capability

Deprival values are another example of current value accounting which we will look at under CCA later.

Distributable profits

Definition: s 263 CA 1985

Every description of distribution of a company's assets to members (shareholders) of the company, whether in cash or otherwise, with the following exceptions.

● An issue of bonus shares (but a scrip dividend where shares are received instead of cash is a distribution)

● The redemption or purchase of the company's own shares out of capital (including the proceeds of a new issue) or out of unrealised profits

● Reduction of share capital

- o Reducing the liability on shares in respect of share capital not fully paid up
- o Paying off paid up share capital

- A distribution of assets to shareholders in a winding up of the company

Realised profits

- Poorly defined, but generally, P&L a/c profits are *realised* whereas *unrealised* profits are credited directly to reserves

- The framework for recognition of realised profits is SSAP 2 with the concept of prudence; following the standards will result in P&L a/c being realisable

Distribution rule

All companies are forbidden from making a distribution except out of 'profits available for the purpose'.

Accumulated realised profits: capital and revenue (unless used for earlier distribution or capitalisation of reserves)	X
Less accumulated realised losses: capital and revenue	(X)
Distributable profits	X

Exceptions to distribution rule

- *Sale of revalued fixed assets*: unrealised profit on revaluation, previously credited to revaluation reserve, becomes realised but does *not* pass through the P&L a/c; this profit is distributable

- *Depreciation charge* where the asset has been revalued: s 275 CA 1985 allows the increase in depreciation to be treated as a realised profit; companies with different revaluation policies are then consistent

- *Development expenditure*: when development costs are capitalised (SSAP 13) then the costs are amortised as realised losses over a number of years

- *Provisions* are generally treated as realised losses

Public companies: s 264 CA 1985

Further restriction imposed on the distributions by *plcs*.

Distributable profits (as above)	X
Less net unrealised losses: capital and revenue	(X)
Distributable profits for public companies	X

Alternative calculation

Net assets		X
Less share capital		(X)
Undistributable reserves		
Share premium	X	
Capital redemption reserve	X	
Accumulated surplus of unrealised profits over unrealised losses	X	
Other forbidden reserve (by statute or company's mem/articles)	X	
		(X)
Distributable profits		X

There must be a surplus of net assets over share capital and reserves.

Relevant accounts

- S 270 CA 1985 defines the 'relevant accounts' which should be used to determine the distributable profits, being the most recent audited annual accounts

- Interim accounts may be used as a base; for plcs these must give a true and fair view and be delivered to the Registrar

ASB Statement of Principles

Conceptual framework

- *Definition*: a statement of generally accepted theoretical principles which form the frame of reference for financial reporting

- The previous approach was just to tackle problems as they arose; this caused overlaps, contradictions, loopholes etc

- The IASC's *Framework* document and the *Solomons Report* have been used as a basis for the ASB's *Statement of Principles*

Statement of Principles

- Will provide the conceptual basis for UK standards
- All 7 chapters now produced together in one ED

Ch 1 Objective of financial statements

- To provide information about *financial position*, *performance* and *financial adaptability*, useful to assess management stewardship and to make economic decisions

- Wide range of users, with some common needs, primarily meet needs of providers of risk capital

- *Users*
    o Investors
    o Employees
    o Lenders
    o Suppliers and other creditors
    o Customers
    o Government and their agencies
    o The public

- Emphasises limitations of financial statements as well as strengths

- All components are interrelated: reflect different aspects of same transactions

- Main elements which affect company position
    o Economic resources it controls
    o Financial structure
    o Liquidity and solvency
    o Capacity to adapt to environment

Ch 2 Qualitative characteristics of financial information

- *Materiality* determines the threshold quality: information that is not material cannot be useful

- Those characteristics which relate to *content*
    o *Relevance:* information that influences decisions
        – Predictive/confirmatory value
        – Choice of attribute
    o *Reliability:* information that is free from error or bias
        – Faithful representation; substance
        – Neutrality
        – Prudence
        – Completeness

- Those characteristics which relate to *presentation*
  - *Comparability*
    - Consistency
    - Disclosures, eg accounting policies
  - *Understandability*
    - Aggregation and classification
    - Users' abilities

- *Limitations* of the qualitative characteristics
  - Balance between characteristics
  - Timeliness
  - Benefits and cost

Ch 3 Elements of financial statements

- *Elements*
  - Assets
  - Liabilities
  - Ownership interest
  - Gains
  - Losses
  - Contributions from owners
  - Distributions to owners

- Any item not falling under the definition of one of these should not be included in financial statements

Ch 4 Recognition in financial statements

There are 3 stages in the recognition of assets and liabilities.

- Initial recognition
- Subsequent remeasurement
- Derecognition

> *Exam focus.* Even if you don't have time to study any other exposure drafts, learn the *Statement of Principles.* It comes up in many FRSs, eg FRS 5 in Chapter 8.

Ch 5 Measurement in financial statements

- *Initially:* record asset/liability at transaction cost = historical cost = current replacement cost

- *Remeasure:* in historical cost system
  - Write down *asset* to recoverable amount
  - Amend *liability* to monetary amount to be paid

- *Current value system* recommended
  - *Asset* current value = value to the business
  - *Liability* current value = market value = value to business

Ch 6 Presentation of financial information

- *Components* of financial statements
  - Profit and loss account
  - Statement of total recognised gains and losses
  - Balance sheet
  - Cash flow statement

  The first two are 'statements of financial performance'.

- *Financial adaptability:* the ability to take effective action to alter the amounts and timing of cash flows so that it can respond to unexpected needs or opportunities.

- Factors which affect the arrangement of information in financial reporting
  - Aggregation
  - Classification

- ○ Structure
- ○ Articulation
- ○ Accounting policies
- ○ Notes to the financial statements
- ○ Supplementary information

Ch 7 The reporting entity

This chapter deals with principles underlying consolidation, equity accounting and proportional consolidation. It focuses on the circumstances in which one business interest controls another and how to account for influence that is less than control but still significant.

Environmental accounting   11/98

Environmental issues are likely to have a growing impact on businesses in the future due to forthcoming legislation, consumer pressure and so on. The management accountant therefore needs to be aware of its impact.

What is environmental accounting?

- Recognising and seeking to mitigate the negative environmental effects of conventional accounting practice

- Separately identifying environmentally related costs and revenues within the conventional accounting systems

- Taking active steps to set up initiatives in order to ameliorate existing environmental effects of conventional accounting practice

- Devising new forms of financial and non-financial accounting systems, information systems and control systems to encourage more environmentally benign management decisions

- Developing new forms of performance measurement, reporting and appraisal for both internal and external purposes

- Identifying, examining and seeking to rectify areas on which conventional (financial) criteria and environmental criteria are in conflict

- Experimenting with ways in which sustainability may be assessed and incorporated into organisational orthodoxy

Impact on financial statements

No disclosure requirements relating to environmental issues at present. Some companies adopt voluntary disclosures (descriptive and unquantified) in the following areas.

- Contingent liabilities
- Extraordinary or exceptional charges
- Operating and Financial Review comments
- Profit and capital expenditure forecasts

FRS 4 *Provisions and contingencies* (see Chapter 11) addresses environmental liabilities (including site restoration costs).

Exam focus. Environmental accounting was tested briefly for the first time in 11/98. It is likely to become increasingly important with the release of FRS 12.

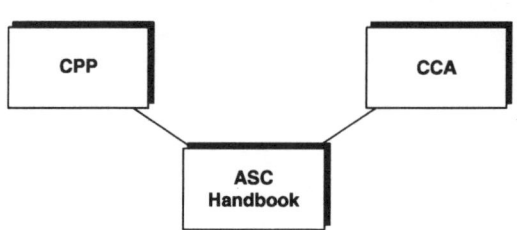

CPP

The idea behind CPP accounting is that all accounts items are restated in terms of a stable monetary unit: the £CPP.

- Changes in purchasing power are based on the general level of inflation using the RPI

- CPP measures profits as the increase in the current purchasing power of equity; profits are stated after allowing for the declining purchasing power of money due to price inflation

Balance sheet

- *Monetary items*: asset or liability fixed in £ by contract or statute, eg cash, debtors, creditors, loan capital; in CPP accounts these are therefore fixed in value; when paid the £'s are of lower purchasing power ∴ no adjustment made to restate year end value

- *Non-monetary items*: asset or liability whose value is not fixed by contract or statute eg stock, fixed assets; their worth measured in £CPP therefore alters due to inflation, so restate to year end values

For monetary items there are real gains and losses made; because the purchasing power of money declines, holding assets gives a loss while holding liabilities gives a gain.

P&L a/c

- All items that are not already in year end values must be restated

- A holding gain/loss is calculated to maintain the purchasing power of monetary items, eg a debtor held stays constant in nominal £ but its underlying value declines: a loss is made

Advantages of CPP

- Restatement of asset values gives companies greater comparability

- Year by year comparisons are more valid

- Avoids subjectivity problems of other current value measurements

- Based on historical cost data so easy to audit; inflation adjustments also very auditable

- Highlights gains/losses to a company as a result of inflation

Disadvantages of CPP

- How useful is the restatement of asset values? Assets now may not represent realised value or use to business

- For reader of accounts, how meaningful is £CPP, or gain/loss made on monetary items?

- Using indices means approximations are made

CCA

CCA measures profit as the increase in operating capacity. Profits are stated after allowing for amounts that need to be set aside to maintain the capacity to operate ie taking account of the inflation rates specific to the assets of the company.

Balance sheet

- All items are restated to current cost; as monetary items will already be at this value, only non-monetary items require restatement

- Current cost = deprival value, ie the amount the business would lose if deprived of the asset

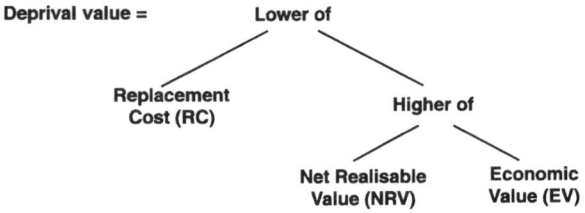

Deprival value =   **Lower of**

Replacement Cost (RC)   **Higher of**

Net Realisable Value (NRV)   **Economic Value (EV)**

A current cost balance sheet would be made up as follows.

Fixed assets	CC
Current assets/liabilities	
Stock	CC
Debtors	HC
Cash	HC
Creditors	HC
	X̲
Capital and reserves	
Share capital	HC
P&L a/c (HC P&L a/c + CC retained profit for year)	X
Current cost reserve	X̲
	X̲

Current cost reserve = adjustment for B/S values for fixed assets and stock + COSA + ADA + MWCA - GA (see below).

Profit and loss account

Adjustments are made to the operating capability of the company. A current cost P&L a/c would appear as follows.

Turnover		X
Cost of sales		(X)
GP		X
Distribution costs		(X)
Administration expenses		(X)
Historical cost operating profit		X
Current cost operating adjustments		
COSA	X	
ADA	X	
MWCA	X	
		(X)
Interest payable	X	
GA	(X)	
		(X)
Current cost before tax		X
Tax (based on historical cost profit)		(X)
Current cost profit for financial year		X
Dividends		(X)
		X

> *Exam focus.* At the present time, the examiner has said that numerical questions on CCA and CPP will not be asked, unless they are revived in a new standard. You should be aware, however, of how CCA and CPP accounts are calculated.

The 4 adjustments are calculated as follows.

- *Additional depreciation adjustment*

HC depreciation	X
CC depreciation	(X)
	X

- *Cost of sales adjustment:* this accounts for changing value in stock

HC cost of sales	X
CC cost of sales	(X)
	X

- *Monetary working capital adjustment:* this adjustment is made to reflect the net gain (or loss) which is effectively made (or incurred) if there are net creditors (or debtors)

Total increase in net debtors over year @ HC	X
Total increase in net debtors over year @ CC	(X)
	X

- *Gearing adjustment:* the above operating adjustments, which have been deducted from the operating profit to account for holding gains, have in part been financed by external creditors; this is beneficial to the company and therefore may be taken into account in reducing the overall adjustments made to the historical costs

$$GA = \frac{\text{Average net borrowings}}{\text{Average long - term capital}}$$

$$= \frac{\text{Tax creditor + LT cred - Cash + O/D}}{\text{Fixed assets + Stock + MWC}}$$

$$= X\% \times (ADA + COSA + MWCA) = \text{gearing adjustment}$$

Advantages of CCA

- Usefulness of information to users of asset values, to assess: stability; vulnerability/liquidity; future prospects

- CCA used to indicate whether dividends will reduce operating capability by excluding holding gains

Disadvantages of CCA

- Getting suitable indices may be very difficult

- Determining NRV and economic value is very difficult

- MWCA and GA calculations demanding; no consensus so lack of comparability between companies using them

- ADA: if depreciating to set aside funds to replace asset, what happens if no replacement, or technological change means replacement is very different?

ASC Handbook

ASC Handbook: Accounting for the effects of changing prices notes that there are limitations to HCA.

- HCA matches current revenues with out-of-date costs in cost of goods sold, fixed assets consumed (depreciation)

- HC B/S does not measure resources employed by reference to up-to-date costs in stocks, fixed assets

- HC return on assets will be distorted by both the above

- HCA does not measure holding gains/losses separately from operating results

- HCA does not measure any gain/loss on monetary items arising from the impact of inflation

- HCA gives a misleading trend of results: comparative figures are not restated for the effects of inflation

Conclusion. HCA may be adequate for stewardship purposes but is unsatisfactory for decision making, both internal and external, eg investment decisions, pricing policy, pay negotiations, dividend payments.

Effects of lower inflation

Distortions will still exist in HCA because of the following.

- Some effects are cumulative, eg on fixed assets

- Inflation rates were higher in previous years and these still have an impact for longer life assets

- Specific price changes may be significant even when general inflation is low

System of accounts

Three main factors affect any system of accounting.

- *Asset valuation basis*: historical cost or current cost

- *Capital maintenance concept*: financial or operating

- *Unit of measurement*: nominal or constant purchasing power (stabilised)

These factors may be combined to give 5 meaningful conventions to provide different systems of accounts.

	Assets valuation	Capital maintenance concept	Unit of measurement	System of accounting
1	HC	Financial	Nominal	HCA
2	HC	Financial	CPP	CPP
3	CC	Operating	Nominal	CCA
4	CC	Financial	Nominal	Real terms version of CCA using nominal £
5	CC	Financial	CPP	Real terms version of CCA using stabilised £

Real terms version of CCA   5/96

Systems 4 and 5 are similar ; the ASC rejected system 5 as a viable system on the grounds of complexity. Procedures to convert from CCA to a real terms version:

• Take CC profit after ADA and COSA *only* (MWCA and GA not appropriate)

• Add back holding gains arising during the year = realised holding gains (CC operating adjustments) + unrealised holding gains (CC reserve)

• Deduct an inflation adjustment to shareholders' funds: calculate by applying the general inflation rate (movement in RPI) to the opening *CC* shareholders' funds

• Gives a total that may be described as 'total real gains'

Exam focus. Question 4 in 5/96 involved an explanation of a set of 'real terms' version current cost accounts, and in particular of the adjustments 'Holding gains arising during the year' and 'Inflation adjustment to shareholders' funds'.

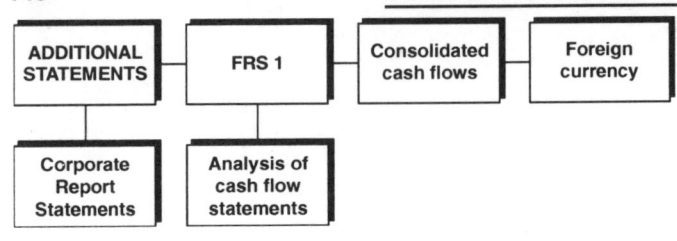

FRS 1   *11/97*

FRS 1 was revised in 1996. Information on cash flows assists the user in assessing company's viability.

- Shows enterprise's cash generation ability
- Shows enterprise's cash utilisation needs

The statement required by FRS 1 is a 'pure' cash flow statement, and its headings tie in with those likely to be used in the *Operating and Financial Review*.

Format of statement

Inflows and outflows of cash of an enterprise are classified between the major economic activities.

- Operating activities
- Dividends from joint ventures and associates
- Returns on investments and servicing of finance
- Taxation
- Capital expenditure and financial investment
- Acquisitions and disposals
- Equity dividends paid
- Management of liquid resources
- Financing

The last two headings can be shown in a single section provided a subtotal is given for each heading.

Individual categories of inflows and outflows under the standard headings should be disclosed separately either in the cash flow statement or in a note to it unless they are allowed to be shown net. Cash inflows and outflows may be shown net if they relate to the management of liquid resources or financing and the inflows and outflows either:

- Relate in substance to a single financing transaction as defined under FRS 4, *or*

- Are due to short maturities and high turnover occurring from rollover or reissue (eg short-term deposits)

The requirement to show cash inflows and outflows separately does not apply to cash flows relating to operating activities.

Each cash flow should be classified according to the substance of the transaction giving rise to it.

Notes

FRS 1 requires two reconciliations.

- Operating profit to net cash flow from operating activities
- Movement in cash in the period to movement in net debt

Give either adjoining the statement or in a separate note.

The *movement in net debt* should identify the following components and reconcile these to the opening and closing balance sheet amount:

- Cash flows

- Acquisition/disposal of subsidiary undertakings (excluding cash balances)

- Other non-cash changes

- Recognition of changes in market value and exchange rate movements

Other notes:

- Cash flows relating to exceptional items
- Major non-cash transactions
- Restrictions on remittability

Exam focus. The preparation of a cash flow statement will always start with the reconciliation note of operating profit to operating cash flows (the first note above). Lay out the proforma for the statement and all the notes, then start with the reconciliation note. In 11/97 you were required to discuss the changes made under the revised version of FRS 1.

Definitions

Cash: cash in hand and deposits repayable on demand ... less overdrafts ... repayable on demand. Deposits are repayable on demand if they can be withdrawn at any time without notice and without penalty or if a maturity/period of notice of ≤ 24 hours or one working day has been agreed. Includes cash in hand and deposits in foreign currencies.

Liquid resources: current asset investments held as readily disposable stores of value. A readily disposable investment is one that:

- Is disposable by the reporting entity without curtailing or disrupting its business, *and*

- Is either
  - o Readily convertible into known amounts of cash at or close to its carrying amount, *or*
  - o Traded in an active market

Net debt: the borrowings of the reporting entity less cash and liquid resources; may be 'net funds' rather than 'net debt'.

Direct and indirect methods

The cash flow statement may be presented using either the direct or indirect method.

- *Direct method:* the components of operating cash flows (cash from customers, payments to suppliers, other cash payments) are reported under this method; *encouraged* because of the value of the extra information given but not *required* because of the recognised extra costs involved in extracting the operating cash flows

- *Indirect method:* the net cash flow from operating activities is arrived at by starting with the operating profit and adjusting it for non-cash charges and credits

Consolidated cash flows   5/97

Extra notes required

- Purchase of subsidiary undertakings
- Sale of business

Minority interest

Only the actual payment of cash, eg dividends, to minorities should be reflected in the cash flow statement. Include under the heading 'returns on investments and servicing of finance'.

Associated undertakings

Only the actual cash flows from sales or purchases between the group and the entity, and investments in and dividends from the entity should be included.

- Dividends should be included as a separate item between operating activities and returns on investments and servicing of finance. (This is consistent with FRS 9)

- Separate disclosure of cash flows relating to acquisitions and investments

- Separate disclosure of financing cash flows between the reporting entity and equity-accounted investees

Acquisition or disposal of subsidiary

Present as a single item of cash inflow or cash outflow.

- Cash paid/received as consideration should be shown *net* of any cash transferred as part of the purchase/sale

- Summary of the effects of acquisitions and disposals by note: how much of the consideration comprised cash, and the amounts of cash transferred

- Disclose material effects on amounts reported under each standard heading reflecting the cash flows of a subsidiary undertaking acquired or disposed of in the period by note, dividing cash flows between continuing /discontinued operations/acquisitions

---

Exam focus. The May 97 paper contained a question requiring the preparation of a cash flow statement, together with a summary of the major benefits of such a statement.

Foreign currency

Individual companies

Receipts and payments should be translated into the reporting currency at the rate ruling at the date on which the receipt or payment is made. Exchange differences do not themselves give rise to cash flows and therefore they would not be reflected in the cash flow statement.

Group companies

The rate used to translate the cash flows of a foreign enterprise for inclusion in the consolidated cash flow statement is the same as is used for the P&L a/c.

- Exchange differences from the *retranslation of the net assets of the subsidiary* will be taken directly to reserves and have no effect on cash flows

- Exchange differences from *retranslation of cash/equivalents* should be included as a separate movement in the opening and closing B/S figures

Hedging transactions

Cash flows that result from a transaction undertaken to hedge another should be reported under the same standard heading as the transaction which is the subject of that hedge. This does not apply to hedging investments in foreign subsidiaries.

Analysis of cash flow statements

Extra information not found in other primary statements.

- Relationships between profit and cash shown

- Analysis of net debt (in revised FRS 1) gives more information on liquidity, solvency and financial adaptability

- Full breakdown given of the value of assets and liabilities in purchased subsidiaries; highlights the value of goodwill

- Financing inflows and outflows must be shown, rather than simply passed through reserves

Relationships can be examined

- Cash flow gearing: compare operating cash flows and financing flows, particularly borrowing

- Operating cash flows to investment flows: match cash recovery from investment to investment

- Investment to distribution: indicates the proportion of cash outflow designated to investor return and reinvestment

- Compare tax outflow to operating cash flow minus investment flow: gives a 'cash basis tax rate'

Corporate Report statements

Value added statements

- Value added is the wealth the reporting entity has been able to create through the collective effort of capital, management and employees

- Illustrated in *Corporate Report* but no standard so comparability very difficult and therefore of limited use

- For internal purposes value added seen as performance indicator, eg: value added ÷ number of employees: use in productivity agreement

Other statements

Other statements/reports suggested by the *Corporate Report*:

- Employment reports
- Employee reports
- Money exchanges with Government
- Transactions in foreign currency
- Statement of future prospects
- Statement of corporate objectives

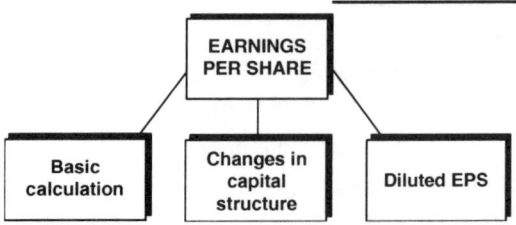

Stock Exchange requires *all listed companies* to show an EPS figure. EPS is a stock market indicator, so it is important that EPS is calculated on a comparable basis, year to year and company to company. *Drawback:* EPS relies on reported earnings; creative accounting can make a mockery of this.

FRS 14 *Earnings per share* was published in October 1998 and replaced SSAP 3.

Basic calculation

EPS is calculated by dividing the net profit or loss for the period attributable to ordinary shareholders by the weighted average number of ordinary shares outstanding during the period.

The net profit or loss used is after dividends, tax, exceptional items, extraordinary items and deductions in respect of non-equity shares.

Changes in capital structure   *11/98*

It is necessary to match the earnings for the year against the capital base giving rise to those earnings.

Bonus issue

The earnings of the company will not rise (no new funds injected); to calculate the number of shares:

* Treat bonus shares as if in issue for the full year

* Apply retrospectively, reducing the reported EPS for the previous year by the reciprocal of the bonus fraction

Issue at full market price

New capital is introduced therefore earnings would be expected to rise from date of new issue; to calculate the number of shares:

* Use time weighted average number of shares for period

* No retrospective effect

Rights issue

For purposes of calculating the number of shares, treat this as an issue at full market price followed by a bonus issue.

* Use weighted average number of shares in issue for the period modified by the retrospective effect of the bonus element

* Bonus element = $\dfrac{\text{Actual cum - rights price}}{\text{Theoretical ex - rights price}}$

* Apply bonus element retrospectively

Diluted EPS

Required where a listed company has outstanding, convertible loan stock, preference shares, debentures, options or warrants.

Must be shown on the face of the P&L and given equal prominence with basic EPS.

- Numerators of calculations must be disclosed. Denominators must be disclosed and reconciled to each other

- Other amounts per share may be shown but must be reconciled to the amount required by the FRS

Convertible loan stock or preference shares

- *Earnings*

Net basis earnings	X
Add back loan stock interest net of CT (or preference dividends) 'saved'	X
Diluted earnings	X̲̲

- *No of shares*

Basic weighted average	X
Add additional shares on conversion (use terms giving max dilution available after y/e)	X
Diluted number	X̲̲

Options or warrants

- *Earnings*

Diluted earnings = basic earnings	X

- *Number of shares*

Basic weighted average	X
Add additional shares on exercise deemed issued for no consideration*	X
Diluted number	X̲̲

* Calculated as:

Shares under option	X
Less shares that would have been issued at fair value**	(X)
Shares deemed issued for no consideration	X

$$** = \text{shares under option} \times \frac{\text{Option price}}{\text{Fair value}}$$

Additional considerations

- Conversion exercise terms for convertibles, options and warrants should be adjusted for subsequent bonus issues and the bonus element of rights issues

- If there is more than one potential diluting factor, each must be tested and only those giving a diluting effect should be included

- Assume all convertibles, options etc were converted/ exercised on the first day of the accounting period or date of issue if later

- No adjustment of prior period EPS for share consolidation combined with a special dividend where the effect is of a repurchase at fair value

- DEPS of prior period presented should not be restated for changes in assumptions used or for conversion of potential ordinary shares

Exam focus. Earnings per share was examined for the first time in 11/98. The question was quite straightforward and involved a rights issue. You also had to discuss the *usefulness* of EPS.

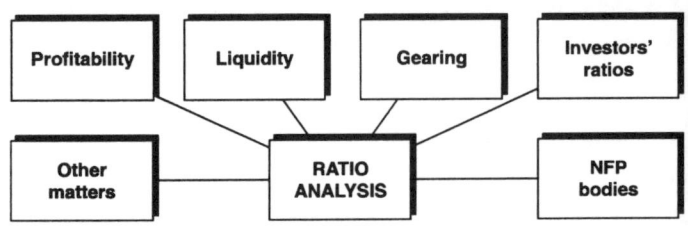

Ratio analysis   *5/95, 11/95, 11/96 , 11/97, 5/98*

There are many standard ratios which are commonly used but variations on these are acceptable if the circumstances require it. The most important thing is that the exercise is done with a clear objective in mind and that general financial knowledge is also applied.

Exam focus. Questions involving ratios at this level will concentrate more on interpretation than calculation. In question 2 of the 11/97 paper, you had to analyse the results of a company which processed chemical waste. In 5/98 you had to analyse a company's performance from the point of view of the company's bank.

Profitability

Acceptable values depend on industry and market strategy.

ROCE

$$ROCE = \frac{PBIT}{Capital\ employed} = \frac{PBIT}{Total\ assets\ less\ current\ liabilities}$$

When interpreting, assess the following.

- How risky is the business?
- How capital intensive is it?
- What ROCE do similar businesses have?

Problems: which items to consider to achieve comparability?

- Revaluation reserves
- Policies, eg goodwill, R & D
- Bank overdraft: short/long-term liability
- Investments and related income: exclude

The following considerations are important.

- Change year to year
- Comparison to similar companies
- Comparison with current market borrowing rates

Return on equity

$$ROE = \frac{\text{Profit after tax and pref div}}{\text{Ord share capital + reserves}} \%$$

More restricted view of capital than ROCE, but same principles.

Profit margin

$$\text{Profit margin} = \frac{\text{PBIT}}{\text{Turnover}} \% \qquad \text{Gross profit margin} = \frac{\text{Gross profit}}{\text{Turnover}} \%$$

Useful to compare profit margin to gross profit % to investigate movements which do not match.

Asset turnover

$$\text{Asset turnover} = \frac{\text{Turnover}}{\text{Total assets less current liabilities}}$$

Measures efficiency of use of assets; can amend to just fixed assets for capital intensive business.

Liquidity

Topical in recent years as interest rates high, recession etc; need to know if able to meet short-term debts.

Current ratio

$$\text{Current ratio} = \frac{\text{Current assets}}{\text{Current liabilities}}$$

Assume assets realised at book level ∴ theoretical. 2:1 acceptable? 1.5:1? Depends on industry.

Quick ratio

$$\text{Quick ratio (acid test)} = \frac{\text{Current assets - Stock}}{\text{Current liabilities}}$$

Eliminates illiquid and subjectively valued stock. Careful: could be high if overriding with debtors, but no cash. 1:1 OK? But supermarkets etc on 0.3.

Collection period

$$\text{Average collection period} = \frac{\text{Trade debtors}}{\text{Sales on credit}} \times 365$$

Consistent with quick/current ratio? If not, investigate.

Stock turnover

$$\text{Stock turnover} = \frac{\text{Cost of sales}}{\text{Stock}} \qquad \text{Stock days} = \frac{\text{Stock}}{\text{Cost of sales}} \times 365$$

Higher the better? But remember:

- Lead times
- Seasonal fluctuations in orders
- Alternative uses of warehouse space
- Bulk buying discounts
- Likelihood of stock perishing or becoming obsolete

Creditors' payment period

Creditors' payment period $= \dfrac{\text{Trade creditors}}{\text{Purchases}} \times 365$

Use cost of sales if purchases not disclosed.

Cash cycle

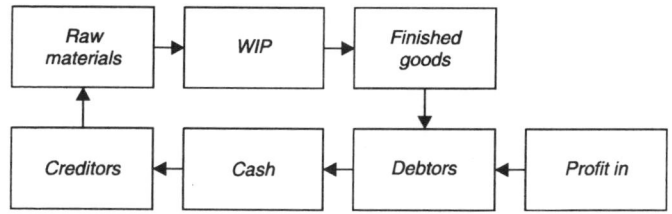

- Cash flow timing $\neq$ sales/cost of sales timing as credit is taken

- Holding stock delays time between payments for goods and sales receipts

Reasons for changes in liquidity

- Credit control efficiency altered

- Altering payment period of creditors: many companies in the recession used their suppliers as a source of funding

- Stock control: in the recession many companies reduced their stock holdings to maintain their liquidity

Gearing

Extension of liquidity; deals with long-term liquidity.

Debt/equity

Debt/equity ratio $= \dfrac{\text{Interest bearing net debt}}{\text{Shareholders' funds}}$ % (> 100% = high)

or $\dfrac{\text{Interest bearing net debt}}{\text{Shareholders' funds + debt}}$ % (> 50% = high)

No definitive answer; elements included are subjective. Following could have an impact.

- Convertible loan stock
- Preference shares
- Deferred tax
- Goodwill and development expenditure capitalisation
- Revaluation reserve

Gearing ratio

Gearing ratio $= \dfrac{\text{Prior charge capital}}{\text{Total capital}}$

Interest cover

Interest cover $= \dfrac{\text{PBIT(incl int receivable)}}{\text{Interest payable}}$

Better way to measure gearing? Company must generate enough profit to cover interest. 3+ = safe? Consider relevance profit vs cash.

There are difficulties in assessing gearing.

- Use of equity accounting to reduce gearing: see Chapter 17

- Preference share ownership by minority interest shown in MI: excluded from interest bearing debt in gearing formulae

- Netting off of subsidiary's debt against assets hides exposure to interest-bearing debt

Investors' ratios

Used by those contemplating investment. Consider a company's shares as a source of income (dividends) and/or source of capital growth (share price).

Dividend yield

$$\text{Dividend yield} = \frac{\text{Div per share}}{\text{Current market price (ex div)}} \%$$

- *Low yield:* retains a large proportion of profits to reinvest
- *High yield*: risky company *or* slow-growing

Dividend cover

$$\text{Dividend cover} = \frac{\text{Profit after tax and pref div}}{\text{Div on ordinary shares}}$$

Shows how safe the dividend is, or extent of profit retention. Variations due to maintaining dividend vs declining profits.

P/E ratio

$$\text{P/E ratio} = \frac{\text{Mid - market price}}{\text{EPS}}$$

Higher the better; reflects confidence of market. Rise in EPS will cause increase in P/E ratio, but maybe not to same extent: context of market, industry norms.

Earnings yield

$$\text{Earnings yield} = \frac{\text{EPS}}{\text{Mid-market price}}$$

Shows dividend yield if no retention; compare companies with different dividend policies; shows growth rather than earnings.

Net assets per share

$$\text{Net assets per share} = \frac{\text{Net assets}}{\text{No of shares}}$$

Crude measure of value of a company, liable to distortion.

NFP bodies   *11/96*

Not-for-profit bodies have multiple objectives, unlike companies. Performance is usually judged by VFM (value for money).

- *Economy:* spending money frugally
- *Efficiency:* getting out as much as possible from what goes in
- *Effectiveness:* getting done, by the above means, what was supposed to be done

Problems of performance measurement:

- How can output (eg of a service) be measured?
- Are assessments of performance biased?

Solve by:

- Measuring inputs instead
- Using various experts' judgements

Exam focus. Question 2 on the 11/96 paper asked for a comparison of two NHS trusts. It was necessary to produce suitable ratios for such bodies, requiring a different approach from that required for an analysis of company accounts.

Other matters

Summary of limitations of ratio analysis

Specific problems with financial reporting are covered in Chapter 28: here is a summary of the limitations of ratio analysis.

- Availability of comparable information
- Use of historical/out-of-date information
- Ratios are not definitive - they are only a guide
- Needs careful analysis; do not consider in isolation
- It is a subjective exercise
- It can be subject to manipulation
- Ratios are not defined in standard form

Operating and Financial Review (OFR)

Purpose of the OFR is to provide a framework for the directors to discuss and analyse the business's performance etc, in order to assist users to assess the future potential of the business. Essential features are:

- Clear style, succinct
- Balanced and objective
- Refute previous statements not borne out
- Analytical discussion, not numerical analysis
- 'Top down' structure

- Reason for effect of changes in accounting policies
- Relate ratios etc to financial statements
- Discuss trends and factors for current year and on-going

OFR is split into two parts.

- *Operating review*
    o Operating results for the period
    o Dynamics of the business
    o Investments for the future
    o Overall return to shareholders
    o Profit vs dividends per share, EPS
    o Accounting policies

- *Financial review*
    o Capital structure and treasury policy
    o Taxation
    o Funds
    o Current liquidity
    o Going concern (per *Cadbury*)
    o Balance sheet value

Exam focus. Remember to address and structure reports/memos properly.

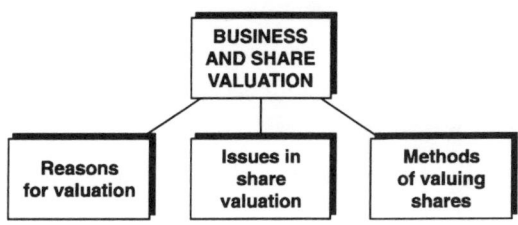

Reasons for valuation

The primary reasons for valuing a business or shares are:

- Merger/takeover
- Issue of shares (including going public)
- Taxation purposes
- Acquisition of a holding

Issues in share valuation

- Is the company a going concern? If not, only a break-up valuation is required, future earnings are irrelevant; the value of net assets is important

- Whose perspective are you basing the valuation on? Buyer-lowest value; seller-highest value

- What % of share capital is to be bought/sold? Premiums for controlling interest (> 50%), participating interest ($\geq$ 20%)

- Is the company quoted? Private company valued at a discount for lack of marketability

Methods of valuing shares

Net asset basis

Most appropriate as a base value for seller of shares, or a majority purchaser if the interest is in asset stripping.

$$\text{Share value} = \frac{\text{Net tangible assets}}{\text{Number of shares}}$$

Problems include:

- Fair value of net tangible assets
- How to value goodwill?
- Preference shares - deduct from the value of assets

Earnings basis

Most appropriate when control is achieved on acquisition (ie > 50%). This eliminates the problem of the goodwill valuation.

Methods of calculation include the following.

- *Rate of return method*

$$\text{Valuation} = \frac{\text{Estimated maintainable future profits}}{\text{Return required}}$$

Represents the maximum amount buyer can afford to pay given a required return, but problems include:

- o Accurate calculation of post-acquisition profits
- o Does not take into account future growth in profits

- *Price/earnings multiples*

$$\text{Valuation} = \text{Earnings} \times \text{P/E ratio}$$

$$\text{Where P/E ratio} = \frac{\text{Market price per share}}{\text{EPS}}$$

Rationale behind the method:

o P/E ratio calculates how many years it will take to cover an investor's original outlay; the greater the risk attached to future earnings the smaller the pay-back period investors will demand ∴ the smaller the P/E ratio

o To calculate a P/E ratio for a private company, select the P/E ratio of a quoted company and discount for the increased risk (by 30% - 50%)

o Where a controlling stake is being sought in a listed company, the seller must be convinced of the worth of selling to the bidder as opposed to the open market, so a premium on the current P/E must be offered

Problems include:

o Calculation of earnings figure

o Selecting a suitable P/E ratio

o Any discounting of the selected P/E ratio of a quoted company is to an extent arbitrary

Yield basis

Most appropriate for small holdings in private companies. Methods of calculation include the following.

- *Dividend valuation model*

  $$V_0 = \frac{D_0}{i}$$ where D_0 is the actual dividend (gross) and i is

  the investor's required rate of return as dividend (gross)

- *Gordon growth model*

  $$V_0 = \frac{D_0(1 + g)}{r - g}$$

Where	V_0	=	value of share
	D_0	=	current dividend
	g	=	growth in dividends
	r	=	return required

- *Stock Exchange estimate*

$$V_0 = \frac{\text{Gross dividend}}{\text{Dividend yield}}$$

The rationale is that the return of an individual investor is the future dividends he expects from holding a share; therefore the value of that share to him is total future cash flows discounted by an appropriate rate. Problems include:

o Predicting future earnings and hence dividends

o Calculation of appropriate discount rate: an investor may be prepared to accept a lower rate of return where he achieves significant influence (> 20%), or where he can block the company on special resolutions (> 25%)

Exam focus. In a question on share valuation you may be asked to make various adjustments before attempting a valuation, or to calculate the future estimated earnings of the company.

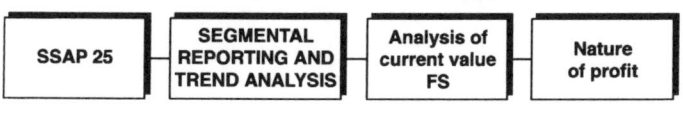

SSAP 25 $5/97$

CA 1985 and the Stock Exchange require the disclosure of segmental information. The purpose of SSAP 25 is twofold.

- Provides guidance to all companies on how best to comply with CA requirements for segmental information

- Requires plcs and large private companies to disclose more segmental information than CA requires

Reasons for segmental information

- Explains factors which have contributed to company results

- Users can compare results of different products year/year

- Users can compare performance with companies in the same markets

- Users can assess future risks and rewards

Scope

- SSAP 25 applies only to plcs, banks/insurance companies, and companies exceeding medium-sized company criteria $\times$ 10

- SSAP 25 and CA 1985 allow companies to dispense with the need to disclose segmental information if the directors believe it would be seriously prejudicial to the interests of the company: requires statement to that effect

Determining reportable segments: SSAP 25

- A segment should normally be regarded as significant if

  o Its third party turnover is ≥ 10% of the total third party turnover of the entity

  o Its segment result is ≥ 10% of the combined result (taking profits and losses separately)

  o Its net assets are ≥ 10% of the total net assets of the entity

- *Separate class of business:* a distinguishable component of a company that provides a separate product or services or a separate group of related products or services

- *Geographical segment:* a geographical area comprising an individual country or a group of companies in which a company operates or to which it supplies products or services

Turnover disclosure

- *Geographical*

  o *CA 1985:* turnover by destination

  o *SSAP 25:* turnover from a geographical area showing external and inter-segment sales

- *Class of business*

  o *CA 1985:* turnover attributable to each class of business

  o *SSAP 25:* turnover by segment separately disclosing inter-segment sales

Results for the year disclosure

- *CA 1985:* profit/loss attributable to each class of business

- *SSAP 25*
  - Profit for each geographical segment
  - PBIT for each class of business

Capital employed disclosure

- *CA 1985:* no disclosure requirements

- *SSAP 25*
  - Net assets for each class of business
  - Net assets for each geographical segment

Associated companies disclosure

- *CA 1985*: no disclosure requirements

- *SSAP 25*: if associated undertakings account for ≥ 20% of reporting entity's total result or 20% of its total net assets
  - Share of associate's PBT, MI, and extraordinary items by geographical segment and class of business
  - Share of associate's net assets by geographical segment and class of business

Criticisms of SSAP 25

- *Going too far*
  - Costs involved in preparation: direct, auditing
  - Problem of identifying: segments; inter-segment sales
  - Problem of allocating costs
  - Excess information confuses readers?
- *Not going far enough*
  - Opt out of identifying business segments if hurts the business, so can be arbitrary selection; need more information to understand basis of defining segments

- o Further analysis of information would be useful eg of assets; interest; transactions with major customers

ASB DD on segmental reporting asks for views on a risk/returns vs a managerial information approach.

> *Exam focus.* In May 97 you were given a segmental analysis and asked to comment on it, ie thinking and analysing rather than 'number crunching'.

Analysis of current value financial statements   5/96

Problems of using HC in interpretation

- *Lack of comparability* between companies in B/S figures: different dates of purchase and therefore price paid; consequent impact on P&L a/c, eg depreciation

- *Lack of similarity* between P&L a/c (largely in current values) and B/S in historical figures

Use of CCA/CPP accounts

- Base ratios on the HCA, CCA or CPP accounts
  - o CPP: adjust for general rate of inflation
  - o CCA: account for specific inflation; create CC reserve

- *Profitability*: with inflation expect HC returns/capital employed to be higher than using either current value figure, as HCA does not account for decreasing value of £

- By accounting for inflation CPP and CCA reduce profit

- CPP may show lower figures if holding monetary assets

- CCA will reflect changes in cost of stocks, monetary working capital and additional current cost depreciation

- Current values may result in improved liquidity

Exam focus. In question 4 in 5/96 you were asked to compute and compare 3 ratios (of your choice) for HC accounts and 'real terms' CC accounts.

Nature of profit

Problems in determining comparable profit figures between companies due to different accounting policies.

- SSAP 9: variation of valuing stock (FIFO, average stock); different elements of overhead included

- SSAP 12: reducing balance/straight line v no depreciation; economic life variation; capitalisation of interest

- SSAP 13: capitalise vs no capitalisation

- SSAP 20: closing rate vs temporal; AR v CR

International harmonisation   5/95, 5/96, 5/97, 5/98

Definition: the use of common formats for published accounts with a common conceptual framework.

Barriers to harmonisation

The main (and substantial) barriers to harmonisation.

- Language
- Different purposes of financial reporting
- Different legal systems
- Different user groups
- Needs of developing countries
- Nationalism
- Cultural differences
- Unique circumstances
- Lack of strong accountancy bodies

Advantages of global harmonisation

- *Investors* need to compare results of different companies internationally, particularly with the extreme growth of global investing and emerging markets in last 3-5 years

- *Multinational companies* would gain various advantages
  - Better access to foreign investor funds
  - Improvements to management control
  - Appraisal of foreign companies for takeovers
  - Compliance with overseas reporting requirements
  - Easy consolidation of foreign subsidiaries/associates
  - Reduction in audit costs
  - Transfer accounting staff across national boundaries

- *Governments of developing countries* can adopt international standards etc for internal use

- *Tax* calculations on income from foreign investments would be easier

- *Regional economic groups*: easier to promote cross-border trade

- *Large international accounting firms*: large companies easier to audit etc

Progress with harmonisation

Current progress, and intended future developments, are taking place on several fronts.

- *IASC:* agreed with IOSCO to produce global SE-accepted IASs by year 2000
  - Statement on *Comparability of financial statements*
  - Framework (mentioned in Chapter 1)
  - IASs: currently being revised

- *European Union*: EU directives have affected company law and reporting substantially and this will continue

- *United Nations*: Commission and Centre on Transnational Reporting Corporations

- *International Federation of Accountants (IFAC)*: to co-ordinate the accounting profession worldwide

- *Organisation for Economic Co-operation and Development (OECD)*: a developed countries body

Accounting overseas   5/95

The accounting systems of the developed world can be split into the *UK/US model* and the *Continental model*. There are, however, substantial differences between the UK and the USA, and between individual countries in continental Europe.

Europe

- *Legal system*: countries have a *common law system* (eg UK) or a *Roman codified system* (eg France, Germany); the latter reflects conservatism and adherence to legal form rather than economic substance

- *Taxation system*: has a much greater effect on financial accounting in Europe than in the UK; values in the financial statements reflect the tax position, rather than the economic position, of the company

- *Forms of organisation*: varieties of organisations across Europe, including different forms of limited company and partnerships of various kinds; all with different disclosure requirements

- *Accounting profession*: varying levels of influence in different countries; auditors and accountants may be regulated separately

Other countries

Developed countries have followed either the IASC *Framework* or produced detailed standards enforced by legislation. Less developed and former Eastern bloc countries have other problems.

- *Ex-communist countries*: economic system resource-constrained; the introduction of market principles creates various problems; instability; passive

- *Developing countries:* economic imbalances and lack of local training must be rectified before sophisticated reporting systems can be imposed

---

Exam focus. The examiner made it clear in his report that, for question 2 of the 5/95 paper, you did not have to know anything about French accounting and reporting practice: you only had to use the information given to answer what was largely an analysis question.

Financial reporting in the USA   5/96, 5/97

Similar in fundamentals to the UK model, but financial reporting in the US is different in focus: the US has over 100 Statements of Financial Accounting Standards (SFASs), ie lots of very detailed rules.

Conceptual framework

Developed by the Financial Accounting Standards Board (FASB).

- Principal objective of financial statements: 'to provide information useful for making economic decisions'

- Conceptual framework should
  - Guide standard-setters
  - Provide a frame of reference
  - Determine bounds for judgement
  - Increase users' understanding and confidence
  - Enhance comparability

- Emphasis on income/earnings for decision-making purposes, rather than asset/liability valuation for stewardship purposes

- The US concept statements contain fundamental flaws (particularly in definitions) but the structure and some of the content is reflected in the IASC/ASB approach

---

Exam focus. Question 5 in 5/97 asked for a discussion or steps towards international harmonisation and an explanation of adjustments required to restate a profit in US GAAP. Almost exactly the same was required in 5/98.

Restating accounts   *5/98*

Multinational companies sometimes reconcile profit and shareholders' funds based on the generally accepted accounting practice of different countries. This is usually US GAAP to UK GAAP, or *vice-versa*.

PROFIT FOR THE YEAR ENDED 31 DECEMBER

	£m
Profit before extraordinary items under UK GAAP	X
US GAAP adjustments	
Deferred taxation	(X)
Pension costs	(X)
Extraordinary items transferred to non-extraordinary	X
Net income under US GAAP	X
Income per ordinary share of 25p under US GAAP	Xp

ORDINARY SHAREHOLDERS' EQUITY AS AT 31 DECEMBER

	£m
Ordinary shareholders' equity under UK GAAP	X
US GAAP adjustments	
Deferred taxation	(X)
Pension costs	(X)
Dividend proposed	X
Ordinary shareholders' equity under US GAAP	X